The Bone

A Novel

by Michael Dominick

The Bone

This is a true story. Only the facts have been changed to protect the guilty – us.

Table of Contents

The Bone

v

My Diary

Everything starts with a name. Even before I could leave the hospital when I was born, they wanted my name. Go to school, teacher wants your name. Meet someone new, they want your name. So if you are reading this, which by the way, you shouldn't be, you will probably want my name. My name is Erin Blackridge. And this diary is not my idea anyway.

Lucy Adams, my high school counselor, wants me to keep a diary. She says it might not help me, because I am not very helpful. I hope no one reads this, but I want anyone who reads this to know I don't like doing this, but Lucy is nice to me, so I agreed to do it. For her. So if your name isn't Lucy Adams, remember, this is personal and private, and I do not want anyone to read this, except Lucy, who promised she would not share this with anyone, or let anyone ever read this.

I don't feel good. The truth is, I haven't felt good for a long time.

Physically, I have trouble with my stomach. It hurts a lot, especially after I eat.

When I eat something, it often results in the runs, but my stomach always feels cramped, so I want to curl up like a baby inside the womb and suck my thumb. I believe babies do this a lot. Problem is, I am not a baby. I am 16 years old, skinny as a rail, and I am a long time away from the security and comfort of the womb. Once out, no way back in. No way. Another one-way ticket that life keeps giving me, without my consent. This makes me angry...a lot. So mentally, I always feel lousy. Being angry all the time makes me scared, and I'm afraid I might hurt someone, or myself.

I live alone with my mother, no sisters, no brothers . My father ghosted us a long time ago. I don't know why, but that stopped seeming important. I just made up a reason for his disappearance that I'm sure is not true, but I choose to believe it because I just do: he was coming home from work one day, stopped in a bar for a beer, met a beautiful woman there (my mom is not especially pretty), and they left town together, never to return. Do I miss him? Yes, but how would I know? You only miss people you grow attached to for a good reason, like they are nice to you or give you something you really wanted . When he left us, I was young and I didn't really know what I wanted from anybody. Nowadays I still don't know what I want from anybody, and I like it that way. Why want stuff you're never gonna get? But I remember him. A little. He was never very bossy, sort of nice to me, but he worked a lot on farms. In my house I believe there is only one picture of him (and my mom) sitting together in the cab of a combine on Amos Kingsbury's farm. She keeps it in her bedroom, but I don't go in there often for reasons I can't talk about.... my life is so unreal, I can hardly live it. Well, that's it for now. I really don't like writing about my personal stuff, or writing about anything else, and I don't feel like writing right now. My life is so unreal, my life is so unreal, so unreal, ...

I can hardly live it.

TWO

Why the Sky is Blue is Because...

Erin Blackridge lived in the small rural town of New Canaan, set among the flat, mostly treeless fields of Rayford County, Ohio. New Canaan began its ancient history with Scots-Irish immigrants from South Carolina, who were fervent abolitionists. They were also hard-working farmers, and the days spent raising cotton in the hot sun of the Carolinas gave them a firm appreciation of the worth of each individual, no matter what shade of color they were. So in 1833, inspired by William Lloyd Garrison, founder of the widely-read anti-slavery newspaper ***The Liberator***, they gave the state of South Carolina an ultimatum: if they didn't end the practice of slavery as the ordained way of life in South Carolina, their small congregation of four-hundred Presbyterians would leave the state. When South Carolina refused, they sold their farms in South Carolina, and left to resettle in a free state up North.

The resettlement was a long and arduous journey, and culminated with a difficult crossing over the Ohio River. The new settlers loaded themselves and their wagons, horses and other worldly goods onto wooden rafts, and set across the wide water. The wagons clattered while the people sang their joyous hymns in unison. After one day's travel beyond the river, the congregation ended their journey, where they assessed the land, claimed their new farms, and erected a house of worship. They named their community New Canaan.

Modern day New Canaan is fundamentally unchanged. The characteristics of the inhabitants and the land they occupy still remain the same. The population has not expanded significantly, but farmers no longer raise cotton. Now they cultivate soybeans and corn. Only two small mile markers dot the highway that leads into and out of the small town. In New Canaan, there is only one five-store shopping strip that dominates the center of commercial activity, where everyone in town shops at Colby's Foods, a small meat and produce market. A small two-pump Texaco station, both gas and diesel, and mostly manned by high school kids, sits next to a patch of ground at the end of the block that serves as the farmer's market on Saturday mornings. Whatever produce isn't sold there usually ends up in Colby's.

All this was walking distance from New Canaan High School. The school sat on a stretch of ground that included a football field and a baseball diamond, all surrounded by farm land. It was a two-story red brick fossil of a building, with six small classrooms, and ancient black chalkboards faded by years of old chalk powder that wouldn't quite rub off. Each classroom was graced with a dozen gnarled wooden desks that seemed to originate from Revolutionary times, and the tops where a student would write were scarred up with holes from pocket knives and pencils past. The compound was originally a part of Lacey Woods Farm, Sam Hutchins's soybean farm, which was one of the largest in the local area. The ground it sat on had been donated by Sam because his son, Carson, wanted to play sports.

Erin was always on the lookout for excuses to skip school. She had a regular list of reasons she kept, and the list was growing whenever she thought about how lost she was in her first period English class. She was days behind on her reading and always days late on handing in her writing assignments. Reading comprehension was a jumble to her, and she didn't like writing about anything.

One morning, she tried to explain all this to her English teacher Ms. Penquill, as she entered the class and was confronted with her lateness and the fact that she had not completed her latest assignment. Ms. Penquill was not receptive.

"There are rules," said Ms. Penquill. "And arriving at school on time is one of them, Miss Blackridge. Rules must be observed!" She glanced sternly at Erin, but voiced her words quite softly, almost kindly.

"Erin," she continued, in a very dry voice, "you are *not* observing the rules."

Erin dropped her head down and looked sideways at the boy sitting in the row next to the door. It was Sinker. He looked back at her impassively and gave her a small wink.

Ms. Penquill, was well past middle age, and she had been teaching English classes for a long time. A well ordered classroom was a point of pride for her, and she was very careful to observe the reactions of any student she was reprimanding, as well as anyone else who might try to interfere.

She quickly directed her disapproving glance over to Sinker.

"Thaddeus Gilmer, don't you believe that people should follow rules?" she said quietly.

Sinker slunk up a little higher in his desk, and looked peacefully at Ms. Penquill.

Then he said slowly and carefully, "People are made to break rules Ms. Penquill… and rules are made to break people…and I don't believe people should be broken. But it seems like maybe you disagree with me."

On hearing this, Ms. Penquill interrupted her shallow breathing to mentally take note of the symmetry in what Sinker had said. Erin was pleased that Sinker had defended her so cleverly. Sinker was her best (if only) friend. It was clear that Ms. Penquill was taken aback and she glowered at his temerity. She lowered her voice almost to a whisper as she spoke, "Another very important rule at this school, Mr. Gilmer, is regular attendance. Maybe you believe you are an exception to this rule?" At this, Sinker made no reply, but simply watched as Ms. Penquill returned to the front of the classroom. He silently waited for the punishment that he was sure would follow .

THREE

Sinker

"What does it mean to be stuck in time?" Sinker said to himself. "I know what it feels like, sort of, but I'm not sure what it means." Sinker had these conversations with himself often. Talking to himself was his way of sorting out his feelings. He talked things out while he attempted to remove another huge mirror from the wall in his dining room. It was very heavy and seemed to be stuck to the wall.

"I'm gonna need help with this…maybe I can get someone to give me a hand," he said.

Sinker lived alone with his Dad, Milton Gilmer, who used to drive an 18-wheeler, a gondola filled with soybeans, as well as corn, over to the silos run by a co-op in Fairfield. Fairfield was a much larger town, with more people, more stores, more large silver silos, and more tree islands on the flat open ground. Then he purchased a used, but more modern tractor-trailer that had an automated manual transmission, AMT, which he could park near his house along the gravel road that split off from the highway. He was getting older and owning his own rig, equipped with AMT, now enabled him to drive longer distances to deliver machine parts for export at the Port of Toledo. Sometimes he would dead-head to Indianapolis to pick up scrap-metal from a recycler to make better money. He was usually on the road for weeks.

This was part of the reason Sinker's mother, Christina, packed up one day and simply disappeared. Milton and Christina settled into their marriage slowly, but Sinker came quickly, before their settling had completed itself. Then, one day, as he began elementary school, his mother was suddenly not there. She had disappeared. Without explanation from his father, or anyone. Sinker missed her, and he often talked about this with himself. It made him feel like he was floating in a time bubble that never moved, like it was stuck. He wanted to get out of the bubble, but he couldn't. He could feel everything going on around the bubble, even if he didn't want to. Sometimes he compared it to a television set, always receiving thousands of signals, even when it was turned off. The sad signals always made him feel down, which is probably why his Dad nicknamed him Sinker.

He looked up from the floor where he had laid a small bag of tools, then looked out the dining room window to notice that Erin Blackridge was walking by. He hurried out of the house to wave her down.

"Hey Erin," he said, mostly to himself, but still loud enough for her to hear. She stopped to look at him.

"Hi Sinker. Thanks for saving me from Ms. Penquill this morning." She rolled her eyes as she spoke but stopped when she saw the agitated look on Sinker's face.

"What's the matter Sink?" she asked. "And what are all these broken mirrors doing in your front yard?"

"My Dad's on the road, and I need to get rid of these horrible reflecting devices before he gets back."

"Reflecting devices?" Erin said, her face converting to the puzzled expression she displayed most of the time, especially when she tried to think hard about something. "Watcha mean, Sinker?"

"I don't like seeing myself in the mirrors, and they are all over the house," he said flatly and as a matter of fact, a fact that everyone should know, and understand, about him.

"And whenever I catch myself in a mirror, it's like a double reflection; it makes me reflect on how things are here, you know, how I got to be here, and where I am now, you know ?"

He continued "they show the real me, I guess, in a life where I really don't belong… and how I'm not the person I want to be. It makes me feel so lost, you know, that I'm stuck, here, in this place."

"Yeah," responded Erin, "I get it." She took a small step closer to him to whisper her usual tweak when she knew Sinker was having a hard time, "Sinker swim?" She smiled sadly at him.

Sinker puzzled for a moment, "I mostly sink," he said dejectedly.

Erin spoke softly, " I know that feeling . It's a hard feeling to get rid of, like all these mirrors. But I think you're just lonely, Sink. Your Dad is gone all the time. Looking in the mirrors, and seeing just you, doesn't help."

"Well these mirrors are hard to live with, and even harder to get rid of. The mirror in the dining room is big, and it's heavy, and seems to be glued to the wall somehow. Can you give me a hand here, Erin?" he asked.

Erin crinkled up her face for a moment, then she replied, "Sure, I can help. I was just on my way to Colby's. My mom needs a pound of butter so she can finish some tarts she's making for Sam Hutchins' Farmers Daze picnic this weekend… you know, the whole town is invited." At this, Sinker felt a little ripple of uneasiness. Last year there were gobs of people there and he felt, as always, out of place.

Erin followed Sinker back into the house and positioned herself at one end of the dining room mirror. She attempted to jam her skinny fingers into the sides to get a good grip. "Nope," she thought to herself, "not good enough. This sucker is heavy and jammed tight." Sinker watched her struggling with a frown, then rubbed his hands on the side of his pants.

"Looks like old Mr. Hammer will do the trick," he remarked, looking down at his tool bag. As he grabbed the hammer, he emitted a small aspiration of breath that reflected his growing exhaustion with removing all the mirrors.

"Stand back Erin, I'm gonna smash the damn thing." Erin could tell that Sinker was especially pleased with this solution. But she also thought about the mess it would make, with glass shards all over the dining room.

"Your Dad is sure gonna be pissed, ya know, when he gets back," she said. "He's gonna see all the broken mirror stuff you put out in the yard. Probably go ballistic."

Sinker quickly paused to think about all the mirrors he had already removed, and clumsily dumped in the front yard. Especially the mirrors in the bathroom, where his dad shaved in the mornings. Then, just as quickly, he looked down and took a deep breath, just before he raised the heavy hammer in his hand. Then he looked over at Erin to make sure she was standing clear of the anticipated debris field. As he swung the hammer, he gave a fiendish shout near the top of his lungs, "I don't care!"

His fiendishness continued to grow in a hoarse voice as he repeated with each blow, "I don't care!, I don't care!, I don't care!"

Erin felt the excitement in his blows, and she ducked as she covered her ears at the sharp cracking sounds of the breaking glass. His blows were heavy and effective, with the glass flying haphazardly around the dining room, then falling to the floor in small bits and a few larger, sharply jagged pieces. She saw Sinker's face reflected in the dozens of split panes spread across the room. It reminded her of a jig saw puzzle she had tried to do sometime in the past, and the same feeling of the sheer impossibility of putting Sinker's one thousand pieces back together again crossed her heart.

 With the last blow, Sinker stopped for a breath and looked at Erin sideways.

Then he said softly, more to himself than Erin, "what I've learned in this life is that relationships don't last. They come, and before you know it…they go…just like these mirrors."

Exasperation filled his face as he recognized that Erin was right about the mess he had created. His Dad would go ballistic. But he also knew that, long ago, his Mom had disappeared, and he and his Dad no longer had much of a relationship, so he really didn't care. Sinker thought of himself as just another piece of furniture around the house. Just the same, he thought, he couldn't leave all these shards of broken mirrors in the front yard.

He looked again at Erin and awkwardly grinned with the words, "Erin, you gotta help me get rid of this stuff, OK?" As he spoke, he carefully loaded the silver shards of glass into a large box.

He collapsed deeper into his bubble as he moved to the door and carried a box filled with broken mirror pieces out to the front yard. Erin reacted quickly to Sinker's plea for help. "OK Sinker, I'll help you," she said, raising her voice just enough to permeate his bubble. She could tell it was the only way to keep Sinker from receding farther into it, but she could also feel her uneasiness rising, and the small shooting pains in her stomach.

Sinker directed his gaze at her and replied, "thanks, Erin, you know I don't think this is going to be easy."

You know something is about to change when your best friend is tearing up the house he lives in. In any event, good or bad, Erin knew she wanted to be part of it.

 Anything fun or exciting was hard to come by in a little town like New Canaan. Odd things happened now and then, but it was usually something that put a frown on your face, like a farmer getting kicked in the head by a horse, or someone breaking an arm when falling off a tractor. Once in a long while a trucker would pick up a load of beans and on his way out of town he would haphazardly bounce his trailer off a utility pole and topple it, dragging all the utility wires along the highway and sending the entire town into a frenzy, with no electricity or telephone service. These events were different, of course, but they were not fun or exciting. The "fun" things Erin could remember happened when she was much younger, when her dad was still around as part of the family. The "exciting things" still had not happened. So helping Sinker dispose of all these broken mirrors seemed like the closest thing to fun or excitement she would get on a dull day, when the afternoon sun was slowly settling into the horizon. It would be dark soon.

Erin and Sinker stood in the front yard among the silvery wreckage on the lawn. She looked at Sinker, who was expressionless while adding the box of mirror pieces from the dining room to the top of the pile. He appeared to be heavily trapped in his time bubble, thinking hard about finding a way out of this mess. Erin could see that even the small reflections of Sinker emanating from the shards on the ground were disturbing him. He took a few tentative steps toward Erin and whispered, just loud enough for her to hear, "but I think I have a plan." At this, Erin visibly relaxed and again tweaked back her magical calming words to him, "Sinker swim?"

FOUR

My Diary

I really like Sinker, not like a boyfriend or anything, but maybe like a boyfriend, which I never had, so what do I know? I can tell Sinker is so lonely living without his Mom. His Dad is away all the time and maybe Sinker should just quit school and find a job somewhere, maybe in Fairfield. Look, it is not doing him any good just hanging around here and tearing up his house. Maybe I should talk to Lucy about him, but she probably knows him. Everyone seems to be damaged goods somehow, and Lucy seems to be good at noticing damaged goods. I wonder sometimes if Lucy isn't damaged goods herself. It's hard to know just by looking at people. One minute they seem fine, and the next minute they seem to be melting, like a snow cone in July. Sinker sure has his share of snow cones, and they seem to melt all the time, even in the winter.

FIVE

Penquill

When you get old, you don't climb stairs with just your legs and your knees; you now use your hands, and wrists, and arms to pull your ageing carcass up the bannisters and railings, holding on tightly to your ascendancy. Abigail Penquill glided easily and swiftly along the hallways of New Canaan High where she had been teaching for 35 years, but she carefully used the bannisters to reach her second floor classroom. There was even more climbing required to navigate the old Victorian house she called home. She had been born in the house 67 years earlier. Now she lived there alone. She had been an only child and never married, so she was quite accustomed to the solitude that only an old house can offer.

The large house was built, as best she could remember, in the 1860's after her grandfather made his way back from the Civil War with a small leather satchel of gold coins he had accumulated from bouts of gambling. He led the construction effort himself, using the carpentry skills he had apprenticed prior to the war. Other local farmers, as well as members of his congregation, had pitched in, trading their labor for his work on their farms. Farm hands were scarce after a war where so many men had not returned. Wood had been expensive in their flat and mostly treeless area, and it took much of the family's grub stake to build a fine looking Victorian styled house with three floors and a fruit cellar. The bedrooms were small, but the ceilings in all the rooms were high, and she especially enjoyed the library room, where the bookcases were built into the walls and stocked with hundreds of books bound in leather, some with bindings stitched with green, yellow and red colored ribbons, as was the custom in that time.

Her grandfather had been a fervent Presbyterian and an ardent reader, and he passed on this inquisitive reading habit to his son, her father, together with his collection of McGuffey's Eclectic Readers. Using the McGuffey Primer, her father taught her how to read. The Primer consisted of a wide variety of vivid farm animal pictures, made from printed woodcuts, like horses, hogs and cows, with their names spelled below the pictures in bold black letters. There were also short homilies teaching about proper etiquette and behavior, and heavily incorporating Christ-centered messages as guides to moral behavior. At a very early age, young Abigail learned that the cow is kind and will not hurt you, and that we must not hurt any beast because God made the cows, and God made us. If we become sick, no one can help us but God. This was an important understanding for rural communities that rarely had access to medical care. The homilies contained in the Readers were heavily adapted for the purpose of instruction, and formed a central foundation in the religious education of many young children at that time.

Her grandfather made it a point to collect books on all topics, that he obtained from mail-order book sellers and dealers who salvaged them from homes and libraries that had been ransacked and destroyed, primarily in the South, during the war.

Her mother had spent many afternoons with young Abigail in the library room, showing her how to catalogue and arrange the books on the shelves. She was surprised how quickly the books became her friends, and she visited and revisited them curiously when she had the free time from helping around the house. Her mother always knew exactly where to find her. She knew her grandfather had salvaged many of the books from dealers who traded in articles accumulated from the Southern side of the war, but still, she was surprised to find inscriptions inside the beginning pages that were written in elegant hands with Southern names that spoke of former owners, like Violet or Hattie Bell, Marcus or Perseus. There were hand-written dedications abundant in books that covered Poetry and Philosophies, some written in Latin, which further surprised her since it was widely thought in Northern circles that most Confederate families were not well educated or concerned with these topics. These discoveries helped her decide to become a teacher, and attend the Miami University in nearby Oxford, in part as a way to overcome misconceptions like these, but more importantly to insure that other young people in the Northern part of America would develop a wider appreciation and respect for the worth of all people.

Throughout the years, Abigail had managed to keep the house in decent repair, mostly by the help and kindness of the parents of her students. The house remained a simple but attractive addition to the land just adjacent to the edge of Lacey Woods Farm.

Although the Woods occupied only three or four acres on the northern edge of Sam Hutchins large soybean farm, she enjoyed gazing out from her bedroom at the thick combination of old but majestic oaks, hickories, and chestnut trees, and listening to the birds awakening her in the early morning. The Woods offered randomly placed patches of green among the trees where nearby families would have picnics on pleasant Sunday afternoons. Sam had the good sense to leave the Woods alone and let the community use it. In the past, when he had kept a small herd of milk cows, the trees were a dependable source of shade for them on hot summer days, and it was not much trouble to locate any strays that wandered there in the late afternoon.

In the Spring and Summer, families would stop at her door on Sunday afternoons, wish her well, then proceed to find a picnic spot inside these cooler, shaded patches of green. Occasionally, she could see visitors at night, mostly couples, and she never thought much about why they were attracted there. She understood that a small town did not offer many places that were more or less undisturbed and conveniently located. Often, the couples carried flashlights to guide their way through the trees, and she imagined that the lights were precious little fairies guiding them to an open patch, dancing and twinkling. On one particular evening, when she paused to gaze out her bedroom window at the Woods, she smiled to herself as she once again saw the precious little fairies dancing and twinkling in the darkened wood.

SIX

Near and Far

The tree branches in Lacey Woods were silhouetted against the fading light, appearing like crepe paper cut-outs pasted on a cement-colored poster board. The daytime wind had softened itself into an occasional breeze, while the early evening settled down into the small clarion call of birds sorting themselves in the trees with the approaching darkness. Entering the woods were the silhouettes of a boy and a girl, plodding steadily together, side by side. As they walked deeper into the Woods, all that could be heard was the low rumble of a metal wheelbarrow steadfastly pushed by the boy while making his way through the undergrowth of bushes.

Sinker gripped the wooden handles of the wheelbarrow and carefully guided it along the path of least resistance over the uneven ground. Erin walked alongside, studiously clutching a strong metal shovel whose point had been finely blunted by regular usage. At each rotation of the wheel, the jangly tinkle of glass bouncing against the metal sides of the wheelbarrow lent a musical air to the journey.

Together, they transported this collection of broken mirror pieces a hundred or more steps into the thicket when Sinker abruptly stopped while looking sideways at Erin. He set the wheelbarrow down, releasing the handles from his tight grip, and said, "I think this is far enough."

"OK," responded Erin, in a cooperative voice. "This spot looks good to me. I don't think anyone will be having a picnic here, among all these weeds and bushes."

Sinker nodded in agreement. He rummaged in his jeans to pull out a narrow-beam flashlight. He shone the light around at the surrounding trees and used it to trace the outlines of a four square-foot hole on the ground that he estimated would be large enough to contain all the broken glass. Erin threw the shovel down on the ground in a quick jabbing motion.

Sinker offered, "I'll start digging first. I don't think we'll need to go deeper than two, maybe three feet?" He wanted to make sure that no one, especially children, would ever be put in danger by digging up broken glass while searching for buried treasure .

As Erin handed the shovel to Sinker she noticed a reddish color on the palms of his hands.

"Hey Sinker, you've cut your hands?" she exclaimed.

"Yep, I guess," he said , inspecting the small spots of red. "Some of that mirror glass must have bit me when I was loading up the wheelbarrow. It doesn't bother me though."

"You better let me do the diggin' first," she insisted. "You hold the flashlight."

Erin leaned the shovel up against her shoulder while she cupped her hands and softly spit in them, rubbing them together quickly to moisten them. She remembered seeing this done by farm workers anytime they had to dig. She didn't understand why they did this, but they always did this, so she thought it must be helpful.

Now her hands were ready for the job. Pointing the blunt tip of the shovel straight down, not at an angle, she pierced the ground defiantly and grunted at the first contact. She felt good at using her strong upper-body strength, even though her dad used to call her a "string bean". She found the ground softer than she had expected, and not dry and compacted.

Sinker kept the light steady on the beginning of the hole and smiled at Erin as a look of satisfaction crossed her face. He watched patiently as the hole expanded, first in longitude, then in latitude. When Erin stopped a moment to rest and put a little more spittle on her hands, he quickly grabbed the shovel and decided to go for a deeper spearing into the softened earth. With steady hands, he began pulling out a growing mound of dirt until he felt a small tug holding back his shovel as he tried to lift it from the ground. He recognized a small tearing sound as he ripped the shovel full of dirt from the hole and realized it was no longer pulling up only earth, but a shard of cloth. He threw down the shovel and whispered, "Hey Erin, shine the light closer on this!"

Erin crept closer to the hole, kneeled down and trained the light on the large square of soiled cloth Sinker had unearthed. The fabric displayed a red and white checkerboard pattern. It included a small pocket with a vertical stripe on one side, and metal buttons spaced in regular intervals. She puzzled a moment as she gazed at the cloth, then quickly looked up at Sinker with an air of certainty and surprise. "It's a shirt," she whispered in an excited voice. "All the farm hands around here wear this checkerboard pattern. I think my Dad must have had a shirt like this."

"What's it doing here in my hole?" responded Sinker.

"Dunno," said Erin. "It's a little torn up, but I am sure that's a shirt," she said. "Someone may have lost it here, but why would someone *bury* a shirt here?" Dismissing her own question, she continued, "Let's just keep on digging."

Sinker picked up the shovel and resumed punching at the ground, getting deeper with each jab. It wasn't long before he unearthed an unmistakable boot, a pair of jeans and a long gently curved stick caked with dirt and shaped like a bone.   At this, Sinker stopped the digging and in an uncertain and barely audible voice, he said , "I think the hole is deep enough to dump in the broken mirror pieces."

Erin seemed thankful at this and added, "Let's just dump this buried clothing stuff in with it and get out of here."

Sinker paused to get his breath back from all the digging and let out a small, thoughtful sigh as he spoke "We better not dump this old clothing stuff, Erin. This stick could be a bone or something, we don't know?" He continued in a soft voice, "We don't know what this stuff is, or why this stuff is buried here. I think we should get all this over to Sheriff Fish."

Ray Vistifish had served as the Sheriff of Rayford County for more than twenty-five years, and was not only a trusted public servant, but a good member of the community in New Canaan. He was also the coach for athletics at New Canaan High, where Sinker had played on the football team. Sherrif Fish, as most townspeople called him, occasionally managed to arrange for athletic scholarships for students to several state universities. Most importantly, Sinker felt he could be trusted anytime he needed to venture outside his bubble.

SEVEN

Dream Catcher

Erin woke up the next morning thinking about things she had not thought about for a long time.

She lay back in her bed and let her mind wander over the dream she had overnight, as if she were lost in a foreign landscape and looking for a familiar sight or landmark to assist in her reckoning. As she struggled to remember the small details of her dream, she felt a gnawing pain in her stomach starting to grow. She did not dream often, and when she did, they were not happy ones. This latest dream seemed like another installment of hopelessness.

She thought dreams were like clouds, as they move along the sky, continually changing their shapes and activities, and all beyond her control. There is no way to stop a cloud, you can only watch it roll on by. In her dream, she recalled being surrounded by water, a fast moving river sweeping her away, farther and farther from the river's bank, until she ended up in an old Victorian house, where she was searching madly for a small nameless object, rummaging through what seemed like hundreds of drawers in an old fashioned roll top desk. She closed her eyes tightly, and continued her attempt to remember exactly what she had been searching for. Her body, still half-asleep, tensed with a wave of confusion as she slowly recalled that she was searching for a photograph. It was a photo of her father.

She startled at this realization, as if she had stepped into a tub of icy cold bathwater, and wondered what had set this dream in motion, since she rarely thought about her father. The dream left her feeling sad and worried. She did not find the picture in her dream, but she knew she could not stop this cloud, and wondered if it would reappear floating gently through another night.

Thankfully, she left her dream behind, and instead focused on remembering what day of the week it was. The memory of helping Sinker in Lacey Woods yesterday night, which was a Friday, was enough to cement in her mind that it was Saturday, and she was relieved that she did not have to go to school. It was getting late in the Spring and she was looking forward to the Summer, when she usually helped out at Lacey Woods Farm, monitoring bean storage bins to detect potential spoilage problems from mold and insect activity.

Thinking of the coming summer made her stomach grimace though, when she realized that Ms. Penquill had already threatened her with a failing grade in English, unless she agreed to spend several hours of the summer each day in the library of the old Victorian house at the edge of the Woods, reading Shakespeare plays. It would take all the contortion her will power could sustain to accomplish this, but she did not want to repeat this class, so she had agreed. Yet, she had every hope that she would be able to avoid this somehow. But as the school days grew fewer and summer days began closing in, she found it difficult to find a way to change this fate. The feeling of once again being trapped was starting to overwhelm her, and she thought about how this predicament had led her to ask for Lucy's help.

Her thoughts were suddenly interrupted by the worrisome sound of her mother's voice on the other side of her bedroom door.

"Erin", she called, "where is the butter I asked you to get?" There was a small tone of irritation in her voice.

Susan Blackridge was a good and unusually patient mother to Erin, but since her husband's abrupt disappearance, she felt it more important to take on a strictness with her daughter that she hoped would compensate for the lack of a strong fatherly hand. In reality, her father Alan Blackridge was anything but a strong set of hands. He had not been anxious to start a family, and when Erin arrived, he considered the event a great mistake that he needed to take on in a loosely responsible way. He never ordered his daughter around the house, never complained about the difficulties she experienced with her teachers, or her unwillingness to learn tatting (lace making) from Susan, a very capable tatter, who often received requests for making fine silk tatted patterns to trim the hats of men or adorn the sleeves and collars of hand made wedding gowns.

Alan, at heart, was a farmhand, and a good one. He was usually gone from sun up to sun down. He especially reveled in the work of harvesting soybeans, and was relied on by many local growers to accurately judge the crop's maturity and moisture levels before starting the harvest.

His abrupt disappearance from the landscape left many growers at a loss. Inquiries at the time were made discretely to Sheriff Fish, but he appeared to be as puzzled as the rest of the community about where Erin's father might be, knowing only that a man's business is his own. And lacking any evidence to the contrary, he had no reason to suspect foul play or to conclude that anything wrongful had happened. The man had simply disappeared. But after several weeks of quiet investigation, Sheriff Fish reported the disappearances of both Alan Blackridge and Christina Gilmer to the Ohio Bureau of Missing Persons in Columbus.

Erin's mother continued at the door and became more insistent, " I have to bake more tarts this morning, Erin, for the picnic at Sam's farm!"

"Omagosh!" Erin remembered to herself. The butter had completely faded from her mind and Farmers Daze was tomorrow!

"Mom, I'm sorry," Erin managed to reply in a small meek voice. "I was on the way to Colbys when I ran into Sinker, and we got to talkin' 'bout somethin'. I'll get dressed and go over to Colbys right away. Don't you get yourself stressed about this, OK?"

Her mother grunted back on the other side of the door, "OK, but ya' gotta hurry. I need it now!" And she added as she went away, "Stay away from that Gilmer kid. That family is nothing but trouble!" Erin took this as her punishment for not strictly following orders, but she had long ago learned to disregard such reprimands. Quickly dressing, she ran out through the kitchen door, marveling at the tantalizing smell of apple and cinnamon tarts baking in the oven.

EIGHT

Dear Diary

I talked with Lucy today. She wanted me to show her my diary, and when I did, she noticed there were only two entries. I guess she expected more, since I agreed to do this weeks ago. So I said I will try to write a little more often, but she knows I don't like to write about anything. So she suggested that I should pretend I am talking to someone I know, someone who likes me, for some reason. And then just write down what I would say. Kinda like what many people used to do. Write a letter to someone you like, or who likes you. But I told her that I have never written a letter ever! To anyone! Not to family, because I don't really have any family; not to friends, because I don't really have any friends (except Sinker). And besides, probably nobody would read my letters anyway. And I have never ever received a letter from anyone! That about says it all: nobody writes or reads letters anymore. Lucy seemed to understand this, but then she revealed to me that she had kept a diary through most of her teen years, and that she never had any real friends or relatives either, so she decided to make friends with her diary. So every time she would write a letter to her diary, she always began with "Dear Diary", as if it really were a friend named "Diary", or "Daisy" or whatever. I thought that sounded dumb, pretending that your diary is your friend, or a real person, but I agreed to try it. The only thing I like about writing to

"Diary" is that I can be myself without having to pretend. I don't like pretending I am someone else who has a lot of friends, and who still has a father like most normal kids. In a way, it's like what Sinker did, just trying to be himself. He was not pretending when he broke all the mirrors in his house. I'll bet he felt that the mirrors were asking him to pretend he was somebody else, somebody that did well in school, and who didn't get kicked off the football team...or somebody who still had a mother, a mother who didn't just get up one day and disappear...like my Dad...and he just couldn't do that. So the mirrors had to go. I am glad I could help him, and maybe my new friend "Diary" can help me figure out that dream I had last night? So here goes.

Dear Diary,

I hope you don't mind reading my "letter", and I want you to know I don't expect you to write me a "letter" back. But my dream I had last night is still coming back to me. First of all, I don't like dreaming. All the dreams I can remember are scary, where I am always in some terrible situation. My last dream, or nightmare, had me swimming in a river (and I don't even know how to swim!). I was floating so far away from the river bank that I thought I was going to drown! The current was just too strong and I kept trying to swim against it, upstream, but I was trapped in one place... my body was paralyzed, like I couldn't move. I felt the water closing in around me, and I was sinking. So I tried to wiggle my legs around, and I kicked off all my blankets, and luckily, I could move again. And I ended up in an attic, in a dry old house filled with lots of old furniture. And I remember the very strong feeling that I had lost something, something that I really needed to find, but then just feeling so lost because there was just too much old stuff in this attic. Then I remembered the picture of my father, sitting in the cab of a combine, working on a farm somewhere. BUT I COULD NOT FIND IT!!! I am not sure why the picture was so important. I remember some of the fun things we did together, like the times we had picnics in Lacey Woods, where I met Sinker for the first time, and his Mom and Dad. I was a lot happier then. It's the confusion that I hate most. The dream I had Friday night was not really scary, because I think it was all about my Dad, and he was definitely not scary.

Sinkers' Mom and Dad seemed to be happy too. My Dad always liked talking with Sinker's Mom. She was a very nice looking Mom, and she seemed pleased that Sinker and I got along so well together. At least that's what it looked like to me. I remember Sinker could climb a tree so fast and then swing back and forth on a high branch like a monkey. I think that was the first time I really felt afraid for someone else. Sinker still makes me worried about things, like busting all the mirrors in his house. And since his Mom disappeared, he just gets real quiet sometimes, and seems to fade away and just talk to himself. Should I be worried about him, Diary?

NINE

Farmers Daze

It was early Sunday morning when Sam Hutchins realized Farmers Daze had finally arrived. He enjoyed working with the neighboring farmers, meeting up to discuss the moisture content of the beans and deciding on when it was best to start the harvesting. Yields always depended on soil conditions, as well as the weather over the growing season, but most farmers could count on harvesting enough beans to fill the local silos before shipping them off to the co-ops in Fairfield.

 Sam could tell it would be a very warm day, and wanted to make sure his place was ready. In prior years, most of the neighboring farmers came with their families and farmhands. His son Carson would run the mowing tractor over the pasture behind the storage silos and then drag two dozen picnic tables onto the freshly mowed grass. Carson would also make sure the steel tubs that were used for the bottled beer and sodas were filled with ice.

Carson looked forward to the day when he would be running the farm, and wanted to get to know his neighboring farmers. The adjacent land to his farm was owned by Amos Kingsbury, whose wife had passed away two growing seasons ago, and his only son moved to Toledo for an engineering job at the Toledo Assembly Complex. Everyone said that Amos had some 'good dirt' and usually surpassed everyone when it came to crop yields. Carson wanted to rent one hundred acres of his land, or maybe buy it, and he knew Amos was getting older. He dreamed of making the Lacy Woods Farm the largest and most successful operation in this part of southwestern Ohio.

It was mid-morning when Sinker walked over to the farm with a brown paper bag filled with the stuff he and Erin had discovered in the Woods. He met Carson in front of an old two story gambrel roofed barn, which had long ago given up any pretension of ever having been painted red. The walk-up to the drive bay was a gentle incline, behind which rested two combines and a large cutter-bar attachment that was partly disassembled. In the rear stall sat a stack of wooden picnic tables that had been handmade from some very old planks and hammered together by former farmhands some time ago.

He and Carson walked back to the stall, where Sinker set the bag down near the picnic tables. Sinker examined the pile of wooden tables, some turned up on end, and noticed the word **Freedom** engraved in large, oddly cursive characters across the top of one of the tables.

"That's curious, Carson," Sinker said thoughtfully, pointing to the table, as if seeing a different version of himself in a mirror he had just destroyed. "I wonder," he continued, "how do you imagine that word *Freedom* got itself there?"

Carson puzzled at the question for a moment, but then replied, almost apologetically, " I don't know for sure, but it's been there a while. You know, there's a little bit of history behind this old farm."

Carson continued, "my Dad says that, sometime before the Civil War, before my Grampa bought this farm, the folks who settled this area, way back, were strongly against any kind of slavery. So they ran a safe house for runaway slaves from down South. As a matter of fact, they were said to be part of the Underground Railway, with this old farm being just another one of the station stops." He paused as he spoke, then continued "Runaways on the railroad travelled mostly at night, and kept close to the water, so the dogs couldn't track them easily. They had learned a lot of songs that were like hidden codes as to where the station stops could be found, and they would sing them as they worked. In this case, they had to get to the Ohio River and find a place where the water was shallow enough to wade across."

Carson paused again and loosely ran his hand across the side of his face. He looked quizzically at Sinker and continued, "My guess is…this farm was the first stop on this side of the river, and one of them runaways carved it as a sort of welcome message for the others, across an old floor joist, you know, from a house that used to sit on this farm. But all this was a long time ago."

Sinker approached the table as a wave of realization and surprise washed over him. He had read about the Underground Railway in school, but it was just a part of a history assignment, a dry and stale piece of history that held no importance for him. This realization turned into a warm feeling of reverence as his fingers traced across the carving, imagining the slow and steady hand movements of the now long departed carver. He imagined the feelings of incredible joy and relief that prompted the carver to declare his release from bondage, and suddenly felt a spark of hope that these feelings could also become his, when he found, somehow, a way out of his time bubble. He imagined that the welcoming message of *Freedom* was somehow, strangely, also meant for him. He knew that "freedom" was a question of "to" and "from"; a freedom "to" do something and a freedom "from" something. In his case, he needed a freedom "from" something: freedom from his bubble.

Carson interrupted him with, "Hey Sink, can you give me a hand pulling these tables out? We need to put them in the pasture, you know, the land next to the wooden fence, OK?"

Carson and Sinker had been friends since they were both on the school football team. Carson was the team captain, the star quarterback, and Sinker was a dependable, if not too enthusiastic, defensive lineman. That was the season Sinker began buying weed over in Fairfield, and selling it to other team members to earn some spending money. Sheriff Vistifish, who was also the coach of the team, was quick to notice this, but he did not want to arrest Sinker. He also did not want him influencing the other players. It was not easy to find activities for the boys at New Canaan High, but even so, he felt he had to suspend Sinker from the team.

He did this with reluctance, but he often reflected that sometimes you try to catch people before they fall, and other times you just let them fall and see where they land. He knew Sinker had a difficult home life, and he wasn't convinced that a falling Sinker would land in a good place.

While dragging out the tables, the boys noticed that Sheriff Vistifish, dressed in his uniform, had arrived. He was a solidly built man with broad square shoulders and a chiseled but friendly face. His police cruiser sat on the side of the road leading into the entrance of the farm.

"Hey Coach Fish!" Carson shouted. "Thanks for coming! Can you give me and Sink a hand with these picnic tables?" Folks were already beginning to arrive and needed some table space to set down their baskets filled with a variety of picnic foods and desert treats.

Everyone called Sheriff Vistifish "Fish", but always out of respect. It was a useful way to shorten an unusual name and it was easier to pronounce. Fish accepted the nickname with his typically gentle disposition, which was one of his key character traits that continually won him re-election in the county for the past twenty-five years. People just plain liked him, and they trusted him to help anyone who needed assistance. He kept order in the county, but he refused to over-enforce the law, and everyone knew that he had good common sense.

Fish saw the boys pulling the tables along the side of the barn. There were still a half-dozen tables left in the stall and Fish was quick to lend a hand.

"Hi Carson…hey Sinker," said Fish, nodding his quick hello in their direction. "Nice to see you boys."

Grabbing a table, Fish and Carson pulled it along to the far side of the freshly mowed pasture. When they went back to the barn to get another table, Sheriff Fish noticed the brown bag Sinker had placed near the entrance to the stall. A stick-like object was protruding out of the side of the bag. Looking into the bag, Fish recognized a shoe and a pair of old worn out blue jeans.

"What's with the bag, Carson?" he asked with curiosity.

Carson shrugged. "I don't know. Sinker brought it. It looks like some old rags or something?"

Sinker entered the barn and saw the Sheriff peering into the bag.

"Fish, I brought that bag over for you," he said, interrupting the Sheriff's questioning. "It's got some old clothes and stuff I found over in the Woods. I was helping Erin Blackridge dig up some poison ivy plants over in the Woods the other day. You know, Erin, she didn't want the younger kids stumbling onto it when they played there. We found this stuff when we were digging," he lied in a convincing voice. Lying was something that Sinker did not see as a fault, or character flaw. To him, it was just another way of looking at the world. He felt it was a good way of protecting himself from the demanding inquiries of other people who saw the world in a different way, a way that was more troubling for him.

Sinker had a bland look on his face, the same peaceful look he always used when he got into trouble of any kind. "We didn't want some little kids getting tangled up with poison ivy, you know."

"What is this stuff, and why did you bring it for me?" Fish said, mildly interested. His curiosity was rising as he patiently looked at Sinker.

Dipping inside the bag, Sinker pulled out the long slightly curved bone-like object sticking out from the bag and replied "Mostly, Coach, we don't know what *this* is," he said, emphasizing the word *this,* and waving the curved object up and down. He continued, "we thought it could be a bone of some kind, and wondered why a bone, and these old clothes would be buried out in the Woods anyway?"

Fish held out his hand to take the object from Sinker, stopping him from waving it around like a magic wand.

"Sure does look like some kind of bone," said Fish, arching his eyebrows. "Did you find anymore pieces that looked like this?" he queried.

"Nope," responded Sinker. "We stopped digging when we found this stuff. Just some old jeans, a boot and a torn up work shirt. Could be more out there, I don't know." Sinker felt his time bubble pressing in on him, increasing the nervousness he had about the lies he told and giving the brown bag to Sheriff Fish. And of course, his fear of getting too many questions.

Fish put the bone back in the bag as he spoke, "I'll take this back to my office and have a closer look at this stuff later. I'm not aware of anything unusual going on in the woods, but I'm glad you told me about this, Sinker."

"Sure Coach," Sinker replied. He was relieved that Fish thought he had acted responsibly, and had not asked more questions about how this stuff was found.

When all the picnic tables were set up, Fish retreated to his car and set the bag in the back of his cruiser. Then he returned to the side of the barn, and lifted a bottle of soda from the ice filled tub by the side of the barn. He thought about the election coming up in the fall, tugged on the visor of his Sheriff's hat, and began welcoming the families arriving for the afternoon.

Carson and Sink were tossing around a football when Erin arrived, carrying a wicker basket loaded with the tarts her mother had made. Carson tossed the football back into the barn and they both ran over to Erin to help her with the basket she placed on a picnic table.

"Hi Erin," said Sink. "Where's your Mom?"

"She's coming a little later, I guess." Erin seemed upset, and looked awkwardly at Sinker.

"What's the matter Erin, is your Mom OK?" Sinker asked.

"I guess she's OK, but I don't think she really wants to come today," she replied. "She doesn't want to talk with your Dad for some reason."

Sinker looked at her and smiled, "My Dad is still on the road…and he definitely won't be here today, OK?" At this, Erin appeared to brighten, but then asked Sinker, "do you know why my mom doesn't want to talk with your Dad ?"

<table><tr><td>

TEN

Triple Crow

</td></tr></table>

The next morning, Triple Crow was perched halfway up the tree next to Sinker's house, coughing and cawing wildly, and loud enough to awaken Sinker. Triple Crow was a full blooded Native American, tall, thin and graceful but strongly built, like most members of his tribe, the Dakota Sioux. Triple Crow was the only friend Sinker had managed to keep since they were in elementary school, and on the days Triple Crow managed to get himself to school, he would stop at Sinkers' house first.

Triple Crow's grandparents had been forced into Indian boarding schools in the mid 1860's while they were only seven years of age. They had survived many U.S. Army incursions into their Red River, Dakota Territory encampment, but were finally abducted by a company of Quaker clergymen and transported to the White's Indiana Manual Labor Institute in Wabash, Indiana, one of two Indian training schools in that state. Eventually, the school ran out of federal grants, and without money, the school quickly ran out of staff, who would have to go somewhere else where they could beat up and exploit little Indian children. Triple Crow's grandparents seized their opportunity for freedom on a cold winter morning, when they escaped from the school. After days of marching through barren fields that were thickly covered in snow, they ended up in the bean fields of southwestern Ohio, and were discovered living on Kingsbury's farm, with many other Native Americans. They all found work on the farm. Triple Crow's parents, as well as Triple Crow, their only child, were all born on the farm. According to Native American tradition, he was named after the first natural objects his mother witnessed after the exhaustion of childbirth: three crows majestically moving through the gray autumn sky. And so he became Triple Crow. He proved to be a hard-working teenager, and was well liked by Amos, and the Kingsbury family, but his grandparents had instilled in him a strong resentment against compulsory education, so Triple Crow rarely went to school. He was known as a free spirit, but also a belligerent learner by the teachers, and no one seemed to care if, or when, he came to school, where everyone just called him "Trip".

Still half asleep, Sinker lay in bed thinking about the word *Freedom* he saw carved into a piece of wood by a man who lived a hundred years ago. Sink smiled to himself when he marveled about the journey this man had completed, carrying the word *Freedom* along the way, and how this word ended up on one of the picnic tables in Carson's barn. He began whispering to himself about just what Freedom would mean to such a man. "Of course", he whispered to himself, sleep still in his eyes "we are all born free…unless somehow it gets taken away from us." His thought continued, " and if it gets taken away, where does it go? and how do we get it back?" He closed his eyes and imagined the carving in his mind, the thick, cursive letters notched into the wood, with the sweeping curve of the Capital F, and the double e flowering into the upswing of the letter d. He also imagined the journeys that Triple Crows' grandparents had made across the high plains of the Midwest, mostly on foot, reciting ceremonial chants to each other in their native language as they trudged along, thinking of Freedom. These thoughts collided together in his mind as if they were impossible to hold together all at once. And then he thought of his own freedom, and the impossibility of escaping from his own time bubble and the circumstances that made up his life. What would become of him?

As Trip shimmied down from the tree and entered into the house through Sink's window, he noticed the chipped up walls where mirrors had once rested.

"Hey Sink," he announced as he looked around the room, " what happened to all the mirrors?"

Sinker came out of the bathroom slowly, tucking his shirt into his jeans.

"I got rid of them," he said in a confident voice. "They were giving me a hard time." He spoke of them as if they were people and filled with animated spirits.

This explanation seemed to resonate with Trip, who believed all objects had a spirit, even mirrors.

"Yeah, *Ashkii*," said Trip, "mirrors can be heavy dudes." *Ashkii* was the Dakota Sioux word for "boy". Trip made a game of blending into his conversations native words that usually confused white folks, although Sinker was well acquainted with a growing Siouan vocabulary, and Trip had been calling him *"Ashkii"* since they were young.

Trip continued, "not only do mirrors show all the pimples on your face, but they teach you how useless it is to spend time combing your hair." Trip could not tame his long black hair, but instead wore it along both sides of his face in two thick braids. He often inserted crow feathers into the sides.

Sink laughed at this, but a look of discomfort quickly crossed his face as he heard the low rumbling noise coming from his Dad's tractor-trailer pulling off the highway and onto the long gravel road that led up to his house. Sinker quickly put on his boots and with a quiet, calm voice, he delivered three short commands:

"Trip, out the back."

" Today we go to school."

" Hurry, my Dad is back."

In barely a moment, the house was empty.

ELEVEN

Milton

Life is complicated. One minute, the sky is blue and almost cloudless. The very next minute, the clouds have overgrown the blue, and locked themselves together, tightly curled in a frown. But you know somewhere, the sun must be shining.

Milton Gilmer secured his rig on the side of the gravel road, removed his tool bag and thermos, took the long step down from his cab and headed for his front door. Keeping his head up, he entered his living room, set his tool bag down on the dining room table, and gasped.

What happened to all the mirrors!

This was the beginning of a quiet introspection.

What the hell is going on here?

He looked around at the vacant walls, pock marked here and there with scrapes and scars where the mirrors used to be. He looked around some more and recognized the dining room table, the empty sofa, and the curtains that had decorated the front windows. He knew it was his home. But the room felt as empty as a soybean field after harvest. The slow discovery that every single mirror had disappeared from the house left him in a stomach churning state of astonishment. He would have to look to Sinker for an explanation, but he knew he would not be surprised by anything Sinker had to say.

His last road trip to and from McAllen Texas had been exhausting. He went in the kitchen to look for a bottle of beer, or something cold, but the fridge was empty.

Sinker must have drunk all the beer, and spent the grocery money on weed.

He opened his tool bag, and with his tired hands removed a black handgun and a thick stack of one-hundred dollar bills neatly bound in plastic wrap. He set the money on the table, and continued rummaging in the bag until he found his bottle of Adderall pills. He popped a pill in his mouth and sat down to carefully configure three stacks of one-hundred dollar bills on the table.

After a few minutes of counting, he confirmed it was all there: 300 wrinkle free pieces of green paper displaying Ben Franklin's face, representing the total payments made by each of the ten Mexicans that Milton had agreed to transport at the sum of $3000 each. $30,000 in all. It would go a long way in helping him pay off the investment he made in his rig. He was convinced that a different life would lead him to a better life, and that this part of his money journey would be short. He thought as he counted,

What do I have to give to my child? An empty life working on a farm... not worth living? Just follow the rules and everything will turn out OK? Following the rules got me work on a bean farm. But now, it seems like the rules are breaking me. Following the rules has cost me my family,

Milton didn't enjoy transporting human cargo, but he was insistent that he would not return to the bean fields. He would not transport babies or children under 18, and he considered women too vulnerable for the long hot drive from McAllen. He would transport only able-bodied men, who were willing to work hard, and perform sometimes dangerous work in the bean fields. And he would carry no contraband, no drugs or firearms, since these items brought convictions that carried heavy sentences with hard time. That would mean the loss of everything.

As he counted, he didn't notice a small tousle of hair, and a pair of inquisitive eyes rising slowly outside in the rear window of the dining room. It was Sinker. Then another set of eyes peered in cautiously alongside. It was Trip. Their eyes seemed to study the room, catching every detail, especially the stack of bills next to the bottle of pills. When he finished counting, Milton left the pills on the table, and placed the bills, the gun, and the ring of truck keys back in the tool bag. He moved his tired frame over to the sofa to lay down.

And just as quickly as they arose, the eyes disappeared from the window, and hurried footsteps could be heard crunching down the gravel road, past Milton's rig.

The boys were moving fast, with Sinker in the lead. He wasn't convinced that what he saw was real.

Trip called out "Hey, Ashkii, slow down a little, OK? Looks like your Dad had a pretty big payday! What's he hauling around anyway?"

Sinker knew his Dad never got paid in cash, and he also knew trucking was never going to make his Dad rich.

"There must have been at least twenty-five thousand dollars, all Benjamins, on the table!" said Trip.

Sinker glanced back at Trip and said in a calm, but tense, voice, "my Dad doesn't make that kind of money hauling around scrap metal!"

Trip laughed a little and added, "or soybeans. And what was that gun all about, and the pills?"

Sinker had never seen that gun before.

"Those pills are amphetamines my Dad needs to stay awake on long trips. My dad never tells me where he is going. He just leaves for weeks."

Trip added once more, "and what was that gun all about?"

TWELVE

Lucy

Lucy Adams was the best counselor that New Canaan High ever had. She was smart, kind, and yet had the strength and perseverance to keep any student on the path to graduation. She knew when to push, when to back off, and especially when to back off hard. And importantly, she knew how to speak Spanish. This was extremely useful to her, since many of the Latino farmworkers sent their children to New Canaan, and she desperately wanted to insure that they would learn the skills needed to seek employment opportunities far away from the bean fields. Her "Back to School Nights" were always well attended, and she received the support and thankfulness of all the parents, who understood how valuable Lucy's efforts were. And they would also bring her small gifts.

"Nos gustaria regalarte una bonita blusa para agradecerte por todo!" they would often say, as they held up a brightly decorated blouse, hand stitched and embroidered with flowers.

On this Monday morning, Lucy sat in her office reviewing the attendance report, mentally noting which students called in sick or had other excused absences, like chores that had to be done at the farm. She noted that Sinker had not yet reported to school, and although Erin was here, she had arrived late, again. Triple Crow was also listed as absent, and Lucy made a note to visit Kingsbury's farm to do a wellness check-in with his parents. Her face tightened as she reminded herself of her previous visits to Kingsbury's farm.

As she thought about this, there was a small tap on her door, and it opened itself quietly before she could manage to say "Yes, come in please." It was Sheriff Fish standing at the threshold, hesitating as he entered, not wanting to startle her. But she could see that his face held an agenda, and she greeted him.

"Good morning, Sheriff."

"Good morning, Miss Adams," he responded.

Lucy motioned to one of the chairs in front of her desk, as he extended his hand for a gentle acknowledgment.

"What brings you into school this morning?" she asked, followed by a, "how can I help you today, Sheriff?" She spoke quietly, in her usual whisper-like voice.

Fish noted that her desktop was filled with reports and colorful crayons for highlighting note cards, and deduced quickly that her work was already piling up for the week ahead.

"I can see you have a lot of things to do this morning, and I don't want to take up a lot of your time, Miss Adams. But I need to talk with you about Erin Blackridge, and her friend, Thaddeus Gilmer."

Lucy shifted slightly in her chair as she adjusted the look on her face directed at Fish.

"OK, but you mean Sinker, don't you? I'd be happy to speak with you about them, as long as you understand that whatever we say must stay in this room. I have strict rules about confidentiality."

"Agreed," responded Fish.

"So what do you need to know?"

"Yesterday, at the Farmers Daze picnic, Sinker gave me a bag of articles that he said Erin had dug up over at Lacey Woods. Sinker said she was digging up some poison ivy to protect little children, but I didn't really believe that."

"What was in the bag?", asked Lucy.

"Some articles of old clothing. But one article, in particular, was of interest to me. I told Sinker I would have my forensics people look at it. Sinker thought it was some kind of curved stick, or maybe a bone."

"What is it?"

"It's a bone". Fish paused to clear his throat. "It's a human bone," He looked apologetically at Lucy and said "To be exact, it's a femur."

A look of obvious puzzlement spread across Lucy's face.

As he stroked the side of his pant leg, Fish explained "the femur is the longest, strongest bone in your body. It connects your hip and knee joints and supports your weight and movement."

"That's interesting" said Lucy, fidgeting with a pencil between her fingers.

Fish continued, "everybody has two of them, a right femur and a left femur." Fish grinned a little sheepishly as he said "You can't walk too well without both of them."

Lucy sat silently as she thought this over. Then she asked, "what else did Erin find?"

Fish replied in a methodical way. "A torn piece of a shirt, probably a man's shirt, one left shoe, looks like a work boot, and an old pair of ripped up jeans, most likely what a farmworker would wear."

Lucy's eyes seem to grow wider as she became more inquisitive, "does the bone belong to a man or a woman?"

"That's just it, Miss Adams. We don't know yet" replied Fish. "I'm having forensics in Columbus look at it. The jeans and the shoe have a lot of dirt on them, so I sent a couple pounds of dirt samples, taken from the nearby farms, to see if that helps match us up with any local operations." At this, Fish let out a small sigh of mental impatience that always arose when he began work on a case that appeared a little more complicated than a bar fight or a speeding ticket. He knew from experience that the sooner you start to get actionable information, the more likely you are to get closer to what really happened.

"Most importantly," he confided, "I need to know how old this stuff is, especially the bone. Plus, there was one other object I found in the bag that may be important, and frankly, I will need your help with this."

Lucy nodded slowly while the Sherriff continued to explain that when he was examining the articles of clothing, he found a folded up envelope in the back pocket of the jeans, without a stamp or a return address. The envelope was addressed to a relative of Erin Blackridge's father, his brother Justin Blackridge, at an address in Cleveland. Fish had verified that Justin still resided in Cleveland and owned a large bakery on the northeast side of the city. He further explained that he had not opened the envelope, but instead, wanted Erin, a nearest relative of Justin, to open it. He surmised it might contain a letter, or a note, or something else of a personal nature that would help explain why Erin's dad had disappeared so suddenly. He did not want Erin's mother to be troubled with this, knowing that she had experienced a difficult time recovering from the initial shock of his sudden absence. Besides, the envelope might simply be empty, and he did not see any value in putting Susan Blackridge through an experience that would renew her anxiety about her husband. Fish had no idea about why the jeans would be found buried in Lacy Woods, or why an envelope addressed to Erin's uncle would be folded up in the back pocket.

Fish continued, "forensics is still trying to provide me with the approximate age of the bone, as well as the gender. But judging from the length of the bone, the old pair of jeans and the work boot found with it, it looks like all this stuff belonged to a man.''

He paused briefly and sent a sudden look of confidentiality to Lucy. Then, in a lower, more subdued voice, he continued, "I am hoping there is something inside the envelope that will tell me more about what happened to Alan Blackridge. That's why I want Erin to be the one who opens it first." Technically, he explained, in the case of Erin's father there hasn't been any evidence of a crime, and no one, besides himself, had even filed a missing person report about him. And he wanted to preserve the privacy of the sender and the intended recipient. In addition, if there was any information contained in a letter that would be needed in a courtroom, he thought it best if he were not the first one to read it. Over the course of his career, he had learned that carefully handling potential evidence was the surest way to retain it's admissibility in a court of law. It would be best if Erin opened the envelope first, and learned what was inside. Lucy and the sheriff would serve as witnesses.

Lucy nodded in agreement with a look of rising concern when the bell marking the end of the first period rang. She fixed her eyes on Fish and in a slow and deliberate voice said, "please wait here Sheriff. I will go see if I can find Erin and ask her to talk with us."

At this she rose, opened her office door, and disappeared into the shuffling noises of the hallway.

The Bone

57

THIRTEEN

The Paper and the Pen

Sheriff Fish nodded gently to Lucy as she went into the hallway, and leaned back to stretch out his legs from under the chair. He noted another chair facing Lucy's desk next to him, and absent-mindedly perused the pens and pencils neatly arranged on her desk, near a crystal paperweight shaped like an apple elegantly engraved with her name, Lucy Adams.

A multi-buttoned telephone sat next to a small potted wax begonia, without blossoms, that struggled to get enough light from the overhead fluorescent fixture. Against the wall behind her desk stood a bookshelf filled with ring binders in assorted colors, and books on special educational topics concerning student behaviors. On the walls of her office hung her college diplomas, both undergraduate and graduate, from Miami of Ohio, as well as her teaching license and certifications from the state. He thought about how fortunate New Caanan was to have such a talented and dedicated student counselor who could have easily worked in a bigger, better paying school district, like Fairfield. Her good work was reflected in the fact that very few teens in New Canaan ever got involved with the Law, and Fish new how instrumental she was in helping him keep crime levels low.

After several minutes, the door gently opened again, and a young figure with a curious look on her face stepped in, followed by Lucy Adams. The sheriff rose from his seat to smile at Erin, and he nodded towards the second chair, gently inviting Erin to sit down.

"Good morning, Erin," began Sheriff Fish, "Thank you for taking some time off your next class to speak with me." He deflected his eyes toward Lucy with a deferential smile, and she returned his glance with a look of understanding.

"Miss Adams says you want to speak with me, but she didn't say why. Have I done something wrong Sheriff?" Erin's hands were folded tensely, as if she were in a dentist chair, fidgeting only slightly with a look of concern.

Sheriff Fish let out a small chuckle, hoping to put Erin more at ease.

He replied, "No Erin, of course not." Then he paused to assure her "Well, first of all, I just wanted to ask you to thank your mother for making those delicious tarts for the Farmers Daze picnic yesterday. They were every bit of wonderful, I mean every bit!"

"Of course, Sheriff, I can do that," she said. "I gave her some help with getting the butter," she offered, thinking of something that would put her in a commendable light.

Fish nodded slowly, as his mind circled around the questions he wanted to ask.

"Erin," he began, " yesterday at the picnic, Sinker gave me a bag of things he said you both had found while digging up poison ivy at Lacey Woods. The bag contained some old torn up clothing… and a bone." He uttered the word *bone* in a slow, matter of fact way, without emphasis. But he noticed Erin twist in her seat to look at him more closely.

"A bone?" she said. "I thought it was some kind of stick."

" I thought it looked like a stick, too, or a piece of wood," agreed Fish. "But on closer inspection, it turns out to be a bone." He paused for a moment, then continued, "Erin, I don't want you to think you are in any kind of trouble, but I need to know what you were really doing in Lacey Woods. Sinker said you were digging up poison ivy, but no offense intended, that sounded a little strange to me. Why were you really there?"

Erin looked hard at Lucy, who sat behind her desk, resting back in her chair thoughtfully. She spoke "Erin, you can tell us. Sheriff Vistifish has assured me that whatever is discussed in this room is confidential, and no one will know. Your mother will not be involved. OK?"

Lucy could see Erin adopt a small mask over her face, the same mask she used when they discussed her diary. It was a definite signal of discomfort at being, once again, put on the defensive, and being given another one-way ticket to who knows where.

"OK", she said. Then she began, "Sinker has some trouble at home with his Dad, and he broke some things around the house and he didn't want his Dad to get too angry. Most of it was glass stuff, so we went to the Woods to dump it. Sinker didn't want anyone to get hurt if they found this, especially little kids, so he figured we should bury it…you know. As we dug the hole deeper, that's when we found the stuff he put in the bag. We didn't know what it was, but Sinker thought you might be interested in it, Sheriff. That's the reason we were out there. I guess Sinker didn't want anyone to know about what he broke, so I guess he made up the poison ivy story."

Fish made a short curl with his lower lip, indicating a small frown, but nothing that would raise an alarm with Erin.

"Look Sheriff," she continued, "Sinker is my friend, my best friend, and I will help him any way I can. He's not in trouble is he?"

Fish relaxed his face and reached out to touch Erin gently on the arm "No, nothing of the kind," he said. "Erin, I just wanted to know how all this stuff was uncovered. Can you remember where you were digging in the Woods so I can take another look and see if there was anything else around there?"

"I think so," she said. "We pushed our wheelbarrow halfway through to the center of the Woods until we found a quiet and undisturbed place. We were pretty much in a hurry to get out of there, so we left our wheelbarrow at the spot. You should be able to find it."

"Good," he said. There's one other thing I need to ask you to help me with. In the pair of jeans that were recovered, there was a small envelope in one of the pockets. It was addressed to your uncle, Justin Blackridge, in Cleveland. I haven't opened it, but since he is your uncle, I need you to open the envelope, and if there is a letter inside, I need you to please read it to me and Miss Adams."

With this, a look of surprise jumped off Erins face and her stomach tightened and twisted. Her face began to reflect a familiar and growing sense of pain as she watched Sheriff Fish unzip a small black canvass bag and remove a worn business size envelope that was folded in thirds. Fish handed her the envelope.

Erin carefully unfolded the envelope and curled up her nose at the musty, earthen smell it emitted.

"It's glued shut," she said with a quizzical look at Lucy. "Are you sure you want me to open this? I barely remember my Uncle Justin. I can't even remember the last time he visited. I must have been barely three years old?"

Fish gave a quick nod of approval to Erin, as Lucy picked up a thin silver-colored letter opener from her desk top and offered it to Erin.

"Thanks…I guess" said Erin, taking the letter opener and directing a small look of betrayal at Lucy. She noted that it had indeed been addressed to her uncle Justin, and she noted his address in Cleveland.

Erin turned the envelope upside down and carefully slid the opener across the envelope's top, stopping abruptly as the shell of a dry and crispy corn earworm fell onto Lucy's desk. She gave the envelope a small shake. A thin, single letter tumbled onto the desk, accompanied by the faint smell of dried leaves.

Erin picked up the letter and in a querulous voice read…

"Justin, me and Christina Gilmer have to leave New Canaan very soon. Milton Gilmer owes someone a lot of money, and Christina thinks he is in some very bad trouble. She said Milton had been receiving threatening phone calls and she saw him put a gun in his tool bag before he left on his last haul. Justin, I love Christina, and she loves me. If we stay here in New Canaan, I'm afraid she will get hurt. My wife Susan doesn't know about Christina, so please don't try to contact her. I have not told my little Erin about any of this for her own well-being…and… for my own safety, I can't let her know where we are until we sort this out. We have decided to go to Cleveland, and we need to stay with you until we can set up a place of our own. I will miss Erin, but I hope we can return home soon. … Alan

P.S. The man bringing you this letter is Juan Benitez. He was a good hard worker for me on Lacey Woods farm, so please give him a job in your bakery."

Fish carefully placed his fingers around the edges of the note and placed it back inside the envelope. Then he placed the envelope inside his black canvass evidentiary bag. As he had conjectured, this was information that might help locate Erin's father, wherever he might be, and solve the mysterious reason he had disappeared so suddenly.

Erin sat in stunned silence and disbelief. Upon realizing that her father might still be alive and living somewhere else in Ohio, living without her, living without her mother, a large weight of disillusionment descended upon her and

rocked her small frame. Lucy stepped from behind her desk
to place her hands on Erin's shoulders as she began to cry.
Fish looked on in his quietly desperate way, and held up
one finger over his lips with a small nod to Lucy as a signal
he was leaving her office. The second period bell rang as
he was getting up from his chair, and Erin quickly rose and
brushed past him, hurrying out the door and racing down
the hallway.

FOURTEEN

Sinker's Plan

Sinker and Trip arrived at school late. They didn't report to the attendance office, but instead ducked into the boys bathroom and continued discussing the events that unfolded when his Dad returned home. Where did all that money come from? And why did his Dad have that gun? Sinker realized all at once that he didn't really know anything about his father, at least not anything that could explain what he and Trip had just seen. Like a sledge hammer coming down on the bubble that isolated him from the world, in a moment's time, he felt that leaving his world behind was absolutely necessary, and the crack in his bubble was so large, he might just be able to get out whole. At last, he could find out who Thaddeus 'Sinker' Gilmer really was, unconstrained by time or the past. Now, it seemed like only the future was important. His future.

At the sound of the second period bell, they slowly moved into the hallway, where Sinker saw Erin running wildly towards the back door of the school. Still crying, she seemed to be blind to everything. Sinker bolted after her, pleading with her to stop.

Erin gave no response, but continued to run hurriedly toward the exit, pushing hard on the panic bar and escaping into the mid-morning sunlight. She was free. The warm feeling of the sun on her face slowed her down, then, taking another step, she stopped. Sinker and Trip caught up to her, and Sinker gently put his arm around her.

Trip took a deep breath, looking at her with a calming and deeply ancestral gaze. "Erin, you run faster than a deer in a fire storm!" he said.

At hearing this, Sinker and Erin looked at each other and began to laugh. Trip joined in with a smile.

Since it was getting close to the lunch period, they decided to skip school for the rest of the day and Sinker suggested they all go to the Woods. At this hour, the Woods would be deserted.

They sat in a grassy patch in Lacey Woods, under a stand of large oak trees, with their broad limbs casting deep shade all around. They talked into the late afternoon, with Sinker and Trip sharing the confusing behavior they had witnessed from Sinker's Dad. And all the money he brought home. And the gun.

Erin revealed the many details of what she had learned from Sheriff Fish, about the letter written by her father that explained why Sinker's mother and her father had disappeared so suddenly. And where they might be living now. And about the curved stick Sinker had unearthed, a stick that was really a human bone.

Then Sinker laid out the plan.

FIFTEEN

Dear Diary

Dear Diary,

I know I have forgotten too many things, because things have wings and cannot be held down by nobody…

I know memories are like stones that are thrown into the river and sink to the bottom, under the water, and stones will only come back to the land when the river floods…

I know that dreams are like clouds and clouds roll across the sky, and they will never stay the same because clouds are always changing with the wind …

I know that even the strongest tree will bend in the strongest wind …

BUT I know that I cannot be held down because I AM A THING with wings to fly, and

I know that I am not a MEMORY that will sink beneath the water because I WILL NOT WAIT for the flood to deliver me back to the land, and I know that I AM NOT A DREAM because I am not a cloud that rolls across the sky and changes each day with the wind…

BUT most of all, I know that I am the strongest tree in this forest and I WILL BEND in this wind until the strongest storm is over.

The Bone

67

Right now, this is ALL I know. Everything I did today was wrong. But tomorrow will be different.

I know that somewhere, the sun must be shining.

I know Sinker is right. We have to go to Cleveland and leave this world behind, the school, the farms, my mother, and Lucy. I must find out what happened to my father, and why he had to disappear so suddenly. And Sinker seems to have changed so suddenly too, and he needs to find his Mother, now. And besides, Trip and his spirit will come with us to help.

SIXTEEN

The Way Out

When Sinker and Trip returned to Sinker's house that evening, they noticed his father's truck remained parked half off the gravel access road, where it had been left in the morning. Upon entering the back door of his house, Sinker quickly noticed that his father had shown no sign of being anywhere in the house. No unwashed pots or pans, no dirty dishes waiting in the sink, no scraps of food tucked away in the fridge, and a bed still fully made with neatly arranged pillows. His father was gone.

Trip and Sinker carefully poked around in the utility closet off the kitchen and haphazardly began searching for any sign of the gun or the money they had seen in the morning. They found Milton's tool bag, but looking inside it, no gun, no money. There was only a green metal thermos with a small dent in one side, and the smell of coffee. But Trip spotted a silvery chain at the bottom of the bag, under the thermos, and noticed at the end of the chain a round chrome ring—with keys!

He looked up at Sinker and with new excitement in his voice exclaimed, "hey Ashkii, we got keys!!"

Sinker looked on with equal excitement and responded, "my Dad's truck! Now we have some wheels!!" Trip responded with a laugh an said, "it looks like we have eighteen wheels!"

Erin spotted the boys through the rear window, entered the house briskly, and set her backpack down with a small thud, on the floor in the mirrorless dining room.

She called out, "hey Sinker! I'm here, and ready to go!" Both Trip and Sinker moved into the room quickly. Sinker seemed to emerge excitedly from his bubble as he dangled the chain of keys in front of Erin.

"We have some wheels!" he shouted. Erin noticed a new look of determination in his face, and intuitively knew that learning about his mother, and the possibility of seeing her again, had created a transformation deep inside him. This created a wave of hope and excitement stirring in her as well.

"But what about your father, when he gets back and sees his truck is gone?"

Sinker remembered how hard it had been taking all the mirrors down, and remembered the anger that rose up in him as he broke the dining room mirror, the last mirror in the house. But this time, instead of letting his anger overcome him with a shout, he paused to look quietly at Erin and said in a matter of fact tone "I don't care. Erin, I really don't care." She recognized the change that had taken place in Sinker, and thought about the changes that were now taking place in herself. In fact, she had only left a small note for her mother about going to the movies with Lucy Adams over in Fairfield, and that she might stay the night at Lucy's house. What was important to Erin now was not pleasing her mother, but finding out where her father was. It was as if her dream about searching through an old desk for his picture was coming true, and she was getting very close to finding him. She looked over at Trip to say, "have you ever seen something out of the corner of your eye, and when you turn to look at it, it's not there, it like disappears? Well that's what happens to me" said Erin… "all the time."

Trip looked at her with a steady closeness and replied, "that's a spirit, Erin. That's how they move. It is hard to get one to stop long enough for you to see them…but…they are all around us, you know?"

"Yes Trip, I know"…she responded, slowly, as if she were still working her way through a dream. "I can feel them."

Sinker interrupted her in a calm but insistent way.

"Erin, we have to leave now…before my Dad gets back." He looked at Trip and gave him the dented green thermos they found in the tool bag. "Trip, can you rinse this and fill it up with water?" he asked.

Outside, the truck and its massive trailer, loomed by the side of the road. The evening was definitely dark, and quiet. All that could be heard was the sound of Sinker struggling with the ring of keys, making a jangly sound as he fitted them into the lock on the cab. Trip waited patiently before he helped unlock the cab's door. Then he looked at Sinker.

"Sinker, do you know how to drive this truck?" he asked.

Erin laughed, as she recognized the look of concern on Sinker's face. "This is just an afterthought," she advised, "no one discussed this as part of the planning process." But she knew that Trip had driven trucks like this on Kingsbury's farm, loading up grain for transport to Fairfield.

Sinker hesitated at Trip's question, but he responded, " I never drove a stick before, and I don't have a CDL license, but this rig has AMT and AMT stands for Automated Manual Transmission, which is a type of transmission that uses electronic controls to automate clutch engagement and gear shifting. This will be a piece of cake."

Trip started laughing with Erin. "So a computer will do all the shifting, right?", he said. "Who will steer?"

Trip continued, "Gear jamming isn't the problem here, Ashkii….the problem is the size and weight of this rig. And driving around corners takes a lot of practice. You better let me sit in the captain's chair and do the driving, OK?"

Erin's head nodded up and down to Sinker as Trip climbed into the cab. She and Sinker went to the other side of the cab and climbed in. Erin went in first and scrambled into the sleeper, while Sinker rode shotgun. The motor shook everyone with a deep grumbling sound as Trip turned the key and ignited the engine. Erin called out to Sinker, "hey, Sinker swim?" At this, everyone broke into laughter. All three were uncertain where this was going to lead them, and no one knew what dangers they might encounter, but at this moment, they were certain that this cab was filled with a happiness that none of them had ever expected would fill their young lives.

Trip guided the truck gently off the gravel, and eased the truck onto the blacktop that led to the main road through town, on its way to the highway. He checked the fuel gauge as they came up to the Texaco at the end of the block by the high school. "We have nearly a full tank" he said to reassure Sinker. He bent his head over his right shoulder and quickly said to Erin, "Erin, this rig will get us to Cleveland…probably get us to the moon! If that's where your father is, that's where we'll go!" Trip's voice was filled with determination and excitement. He was glad to be behind the wheel and on the road with the two people in this world he could call his friends. As he spoke, Erin felt the words filter inside her mind like visitors from a long ago dream she could barely remember. She straightened up from the sleeper and stared out the front windshield of the truck. It was late at night, everything was closed and only the streetlight in front of Colby's Food Market flickered in the dark like an aging comet. She began to feel the comfort of the deep rumble of the truck engine as the gears changed, lowering the clutch plates into slower revolutions as the truck gained speed. Sinker slowly turned in his seat to look at her, fastening his stare on her face as if he had never understood who she was before…as if this were the first time he had ever noticed the real Erin Blackridge…as if he were also a visitor from the dream she could not quite recall. He shifted his head closer to her and smiled protectively at her, and she smiled back, with a knowing feeling that he would have a place in that dream. As the big gear jolted the truck into cruising speed, she rocked forward with the transition, and gently placed her lips together with Sinker's. Now both were in the same dream, lips together, eyes closed. At that moment, her memories broke loose inside her, like cargo rolling unhinged in the empty trailer behind her, and she remembered how she lost the balloon filled with floating gas that her father gave her at the county fair. Large and red and floating, with a white string wrapped around her wrist, that somehow came unmoored and just went up and up, higher and higher into the blue summer sky, with no way to stop it or ever getting it back. She had not cried at this, but had felt only excitement for the balloon, and her intense wonderment at the curious flight that had begun so unexpectedly and that appeared would never end.

Paco's Story

Paco Sendero was born in the town of Pueblo Molino in the Mexican state of Chihuahua, an area that used to be called "El Paso del Norte." The small community in the town was devoutly Catholic, and a life size crucifix of Jesus was firmly affixed to the highest boulder set into the rugged hillsides that surrounded the town. Paco was a gentle boy, who loved working with the goats, pigs and chickens his father raised to bring in the small amounts of money needed to provide for the family, and when he finished his third grade, he was recruited to serve as an altar boy at Sangre de Cristo church.

And so it was, when he was seventeen, and on his way home from Sunday church services, Paco saw two heavily tattooed men waiting at the door, smoking cigarettes below the second floor window of his home. One was tall, one was short. Paco could see the shiny pistol poking out from the waistband of the short man who had the initials BA tattooed in large block letters on his forearm. Paco considered returning to the church, but then continued on towards the men. His father had warned him that this day might come, when tattooed men would arrive at his door and demand that he join their gang. The short man saw Paco coming and called out to him in a tired, dismissive manner, "OK Paco, you gotta come with us, time to join up with your friends. No more of this church stuff with Father Diego…time to be a man."

Paco continued to approach the men but stopped when he heard the scraping noise of the upstairs window slowly opening. He looked up and saw his father leaning out the window, holding a large round cooking pot with a cloud of steam rising off the rim. In an instant, the pot was turned upside down, and the boiling water was cascading through the still Sunday morning air, loudly hissing as it hit the face of the short man who had also been looking up at the sound of the window opening. The screams of the short man terrified the neighborhood, while his father shouted back with commands and invectives that his son would never join Barrio Azteca.

"Never !

Barrio Azteca (BA) first emerged in the prisons of El Paso, Texas, in the 1980s. After serving their sentences, prisoners were deported across the border to Mexico and other Central American countries. It expanded its influence in the border region by striking alliances with Mexican drug trafficking networks, above all, the Juarez Cartel.

Within two days, other members of BA reappeared at Paco's door, and executed his father in front of his mother. They promised to return and shoot both Paco and his mother if Paco did not join the gang . This is how Paco was forced into a gang. The money he was promised as a gang member was unimportant to him, as he had always been satisfied with his young life, impoverished as it was.

Coming of age in a poor household was all he ever expected.

The money he made was always sent to his widowed mother, who had no other source of income. He had many opportunities to reflect on the difficult path his life had now taken as a gang member. But in these reflections, he kept returning to the feeling that he had been caught in the maw of life, the eternal recycling of the pain and suffering that was present everywhere. And he had no way out.

So he became a truck driver for the Aztecans, trafficking human cargo, mostly migrants, into the parts of the United States that needed the cheap labor that immigrants could provide. He would drive an 18-wheeler filled with auto parts, manufactured in Matamoros, across the border into Brownsville, Texas. The purpose of that part of the trip was to successfully pass through the border inspections performed by the U.S. Border Patrol, so he could get the truck into the country cleanly for the purpose of transporting human cargo. This is why he never transported cocaine or other drugs, which would be easily discovered by canine handlers. If discovered, Paco would lose the truck, and the gang would lose another trafficker. The gangs had other ways of smuggling drugs, and other types of contraband.

Once in the U.S., he would deliver the auto parts to other carriers and then drive his empty truck for a layover in Muleshoe, a sparsely inhabited agricultural and cattle-raising town in the high plains of West Texas. Muleshoe was a good place to hide people and stay out of the way of Immigration and Customs Enforcement police.

In Muleshoe, another gang member would be waiting for Paco with a group of two dozen immigrants, ready to be loaded into the truck, after making payments averaging $5000 each. Hauling people is hard work, and preparing the truck and the human cargo for the ride to somewhere in the Midwest of America is more complicated than hauling auto parts. But there is big money in it, particularly if you are hauling immigrants who will work on farms. Farm Labor Contractors based in the United States were often abusive with the immigrants, frequently enslaving them by conspiring with farmers to steal their documents and wages.

This peril was widely known by potential immigrants, who would then choose to get to farms by going with independent traffickers like Paco and his gang to avoid being enslaved. Sometimes Paco would load entire families onto the mattresses that covered the floor of his truck, including babies, babies who needed diapers and feeding. And supplying food and water for the long trip north was always a problem. Some of the anxious immigrants would hoard the plastic water bottles and fights would break out. And there is no letting anyone out for a bathroom break. Plastic buckets behind a tarp strung up along the wooden side rails of the truck would do.

Most of his trips north were scheduled for the early spring to avoid the problems of being on the road in hot summer conditions. The trucks he drove did not have air-conditioning.

But sometimes there were particular demands for immigrants in the hot months, harvesting strawberries and cherries, but Paco had no control over the orders he received from the boss, the Word One, the *Palabra Uno*. He had been lucky for the first few trips he made through the summer heat. When he arrived at the designated location and opened the rear doors, everyone was still alive, often barely. But the operations were well organized, and the gang member who organized the drop sites always kept body bags and a back hoe available for the disposition of dead bodies. The gang always made sure there were no loose ends.

And so it happened that on one of his trips to south-western Ohio, he delivered a group of migrants for work in the bean fields on Lacey Woods Farm. This was Sam Hutchin's farm, and heavy rains that year insured a harvest that required many new farm workers. Upon arrival, Sam would meet the truck and select the most able bodies available, and Paco assured Sam that, for a price, he would deliver as many new workers as Sam required. This represented a new income stream for the Barrio Aztecans, and Paco was rewarded with new responsibilities and placed in charge of business development in the upper Midwest. With this, Paco sensed he had opened up a new promising opportunity for himself, where he would no longer be required to drive the truck and face the risk of being jailed for the rest of his life. But he would need to find a new driver, preferably an American. It did not take long before his sources in Matamoros recruited Milton Gilmer. And for Milton, it seemed as if a new door was opening, and so, he walked through it. But he reflected…what was on the other side?

EIGHTEEN

Parents and Children

What is a parent? What does it mean to be a parent? What is a child? What does it mean to be a child?

In the deep of night, Trip steered the truck gently around the bends in the highway, and was careful not to wake Erin as she rested in the sleeper of the cab. But she could not really find sleep. The closer they came to Cleveland, the more her excitement grew. Questions about parents and children kept running through her mind. She had never thought about these questions before now. Before the now that was bringing her closer to reuniting with a parent that she had not seen for years. But was her father really alive and well in Cleveland? She had never imagined that she would ever see him again. Over the years of his absence, she had imagined many different things that could have happened to him, but they mostly funneled down to one conclusion: *he was dead.* And didn't Sheriff Fish tell her that she and Sinker had found a bone, that night, buried in Lacey Woods. And wasn't there a letter in the pocket of the jeans, a letter written by her father? Could the bone possibly be all that remained of her father? Did she somehow discover through pure happenstance, what had happened to her father all those years ago?

She realized that for Sinker, it must be the same set of feelings that kept him so quiet. She wondered …"is missing a mother more painful than missing a father? Do you really need *two* parents."

Erin had lived without her father for most of her elementary school years, without many repercussions. Her mother was good to her, mostly understanding that little Erin was growing up without her dad. Not having him around made the house seem bigger, and less messy. No work gloves or sweat-filled cotton bandanas randomly strewn around the living room. No clumps of dirt falling off his work boots, dragged around on the carpet as he came into the house late after the evening meal was over. She like to pretend this was normal behavior for a field hand on Sam Hutchin's farm, even though her mother never failed to continually complain, "Why can't your father take off his boots before he enters the house?"

She liked to pretend that it was a blessing not having to listen to the futile arguments and small bickering that her parents regularly engaged in. Although their fights became more frequent before his disappearance, she never tried to pay much attention, or give it much importance. But now she thought, *"what does a child understand about her parents. Are they just two grown ups, older people, who live in the same place, with the same partner, and the same child ?"*

"But do they really live in the same place? My father went to the fields every day, from early in the morning, until the sun set behind Amos Kingsbury's large silver silo. He didn't come back home until well after me and my mom had finished our dinners. And mom spent most of her day

sewing dresses and tatting hats, and patching up and rescuing all sorts of clothing that people in our farming community were too frugal, or too poor, to throw away. She would usually work on our front porch when the weather was nice, ready to welcome new customers who needed her services. This contrasts harshly with my father working in the bean fields, often in the hot sun, or the icy rain, driving heavy machinery and directing laborers on the proper way to fertilize acres of crops by dispensing chemicals and pesticides that are harmful to humans."

It became clear to Erin that, through all these years, her parents had not really lived in the same place after all. In reality, she realized their separation had been ongoing for a long time, long before her father had actually disappeared. She thought, *"how long was he really here? When did he really disappear?"* But the questions she insisted on pursuing in the years after he first disappeared, the questions that seemed to be unanswerable, maybe unknowable to a six year old child was *"Where is my father? What made him disappear? Why did he leave me? I remember falling down the stairs at home when I was little and my Dad came to pick me up. Nothing broken, only bruised... I don't remember how it happened. But he was there, and I remember his strong arms surrounding me as I lay on the floor, picking me up, and I remember the smell of his freshly washed, soft cotton work shirt that he wore when he worked in the bean fields. My arms never wanted to let go of him...but I never expected he would let go of me."*

Now, with the advantage of her growing awareness of how the real world works, the answers to these very important questions suddenly became more complex to her, more nuanced, and began to reveal themselves in a more understandable way. She now felt closer to her father than she could ever remember. She could feel the love for her father gently awakening and blossoming in her heart, a heart that had been repressed in anger and loss for such a long time.

NINETEEN

P. L. S.

"Ghosts are real. Ghosts exist. They are all around us," said Abigail Penquill, her voice worked up and filled with concern. She continued, "Shakespeare wrote a play he called *Hamlet*. And one of the first characters in the play is a ghost, a ghost who had been a king, and who happened to be Hamlet's father. Hamlet was informed by this ghost that his father was murdered by his brother, who was having a love affair with Hamlet's mother, the Queen Gertrude. So Hamlet spent the rest of his young life trying to prove that his uncle and his mother were responsible for his father's disappearance from his life." Ms. Penquill looked at Lucy Adams with a worried but insistent stare, as if she had just discovered the truth about the disappearance of Erin's father. Lucy twisted subtly in her chair on the other side of the desk. Lucy deflected Ms. Penquill's gaze by looking at Susan Blackridge, who was seated in the chair next to her. Lucy had asked Susan to meet with her at school to explain what happened yesterday when Erin had learned about the circumstances of her father's disappearance. And because Ms. Penquill had so many concerns about Erin, she had invited herself to the meeting. Lucy had reluctantly agreed to include her when she learned that Erin had not shown up at school that day, and when Susan said Erin had not been back home for the night.

Now the three women sat uncomfortably in Lucy's office hoping one of them knew where Erin was.

Lucy interrupted the hollow silence and began to relate the details of yesterday's meeting with Sherrif Fish. She recounted the episode about Erin and Sinker digging a hole at night in Lacey Woods, and finding the old clothing and the mysterious bone. She related the information contained in the letter found in the worn clothing about Susan's husband and Sinker's mom, and their intention of departing for Cleveland to necessarily protect their families. Susan Blackridge did not seem surprised at the news. "Lucy", she began, "I had some reasons to believe there was a connection between them, but I knew there was nothing I could do. So I didn't say anything at the time because I didn't want Erin to know, but it looks like she found out from a ghost in Lacey Woods."

Ms. Penquill nodded in agreement.

Susan continued, "Erin told me she was going to a movie with you over in Fairfield, and if it were late, she would stay at your home for the night."

"No Susan, I'm afraid that's not right. I haven't seen her since she ran out of school yesterday, after our meeting. She is probably on her way to Cleveland, with Sinker, to look for her father."

Susan looked down at her hands that were folded in her lap. Her wedding ring still remained in its proper place. With a muffled tear catching in her voice she said "I don't know how all of this happened. I never wanted little Erin to find out."

Ms. Penquill reached out to touch her shoulder softly and offered in a calming voice "Susan, people change. Over time. It is not that they don't love you anymore. It's just that they don't like *themselves* anymore, they don't like what or who they've become, and they want to change that. So they begin the process of separating themselves from their current life, and start exploring the world around them for a new incarnation." She took a Kleenex from the box on Lucy's desk and passed it to Susan. After a small pause, she continued "Leaving your spouse is like a process of reincarnation, becoming someone new. Sometimes it takes a while to do this; sometimes it can happen suddenly, for example, with a chance encounter with someone they have never met before."

Ms. Penquill took a deeper breath and exhaled with a sigh before continuing "One thing we know for sure… like Hamlet, Erin is an extraordinarily strong willed young girl, and she wants to find out what happened to her father. So I believe she is on her way with Sinker to Cleveland, to find their missing parents." Then she paused before she said, "So Lucy,…you and I are going to Cleveland to look out for those kids. But we must remember one thing…Susan, your husband may not be in Cleveland. He may be dead. And learning this will be crushing for Erin."

TWENTY

On the Road Again

Milton Gilmer returned home late that night to discover his truck was no longer parked on the edge of the gravel road, and in its place, sat the official cruiser of Sheriff Fish. Milton walked up to the car and saw Sheriff Fish, eyes closed, quietly resting behind the wheel. Milton tapped softly on the window. Sheriff Fish opened his eyes and rolled it down.

Milton spoke in a scratchy voice, filled with a quiet exasperation.

" Good evening, Sheriff, fancy to see you here, so late at night. Maybe you heard? Someone took my truck. You don't happen to know what happened to it, do you?"

Sheriff unlocked the doors of his squad car.

"Mr. Gilmer, better get in the car…please," responded Fish.

Milton recognized a polite but firm directive in Fish's request. He ducked his head as he slowly got in and sat on the passenger side of the front seat.

"I am not sure where your truck is right now," said Fish, "but you and I are gonna find out. Milton, we are going to Cleveland."

The sheriff started up his car and slid back off the gravel, heading back to the main highway toward interstate 71 and Cleveland. He was glad he had run by Milton's house and confirmed his hunch: that Sinker had stolen his father's truck and both Erin and Sinker were on their way to Cleveland , to find their missing parents. He also needed the opportunity to speak with Milton and confirm the contents of the letter that was found in the old clothes.

Fish looked over at Milton and began the conversation in a quiet way.

"Milt, I need to have a difficult conversation with you about your wife. Maybe you know this, or, maybe you don't."

Milton slouched a little lower in his seat.

"You know, Sheriff, my wife left me some years ago, and I haven't heard from her since. So I really don't know a lot about what she is up to these days."

Fish began patiently. "Well, a few nights ago Erin and your boy dug up some stuff over in Lacey Woods. Mixed in with that stuff was a note that gives us the information that your wife was romantically involved with Alan Blackridge, who is Erin's Dad. He disappeared, as you know, several years ago, about the same time your wife did, and nobody really knows what happened to them."

"That's true, Sheriff…but what's that got to do with me?"

"Milt… didn't she ever talk to you about it?"

"I've been on the road a lot these past few years, you know, after I bought the new truck. That's why I've got to find it soon because I have a few more runs to make. I still have a note to pay off."

"I understand," said the Sheriff, nodding. "What are you hauling around these days?"

Milt shifted more in his seat and asked "Sheriff, do you have any coffee in the car… 'cause I'm getting a little sleepy here tonight."

"I'm sorry Milt… I don't usually need coffee at night. Get some when we stop for gas, OK?"

"OK." Milton stretched a little to look over at the fuel gauge. It showed about half-a-tank.

"Are we really going to Cleveland?" he asked.

"Hopefully, we're going to find your truck, to be sure. And we're going to find your boy Sinker and his friend Erin. I have reason to believe they are both in Cleveland, looking for Erin's Dad…and your wife."

Milton let out a small puff of air with a "Jeez" attached. He looked over at the Sheriff with a sad, perplexed face. "Why would they be in Cleveland, Sheriff?"

Fish held his response to this question, preferring instead to keep his eye on the turnpike while the mile markers kept their steady countdown on the number of miles to Cleveland. He gazed up through his windshield at a large yellow half-moon, hanging over a thick clump of loblolly pines off in the distance. He glanced over at Milton, who was lost in his own thoughts, as if this ride-along with the County Sheriff was quite an ordinary event.

"Milton, your boy and his friend Erin were out digging in Lacey Woods the other night, trying to bury some stuff he destroyed in your house. In the digging, they uncovered an old pair of jeans. Inside one of the pockets, they found a letter that indicated your wife and Alan Blackridge 'might' be heading for Cleveland. It was a letter that was addressed to Alan Blackridge's older brother, who lives in Cleveland." The Sheriff paused for a moment to see how Milton was taking the news. Then he continued, "I say they 'might' have been heading to Cleveland only because the letter was found in the back pocket of the buried jeans. And that means it was never delivered. And since it was never delivered, Blackridge and your wife may not have made it to Cleveland. They may have *intended* to go to Cleveland, but I still don't really know where they are, or even if they are still alive."

Fish glanced over at Milton to get some reaction. Then he added "Milton…there was something else that was buried near the same place where the kids found the jeans…" and he paused. "They also found a bone."

Milton twisted in his seat slightly to look closer at the Sheriff.

"What kind of bone?" he asked.

"It's a human bone. Looks like part of somebody's leg," replied Fish.

Milton arched his eyebrows. "How did a human bone get buried in Lacy Woods?" He looked genuinely puzzled at this, and continued "I guess that's why you got involved in all this, huh Sheriff? Is that the reason we are heading to Cleveland?"

Fish glanced quickly at Milton, "Well, I sure do have a lot of questions. Trouble is, I don't have a lot of answers. But I have to find your truck, and those kids. And it would be nice to find Alan Blackridge and your wife, if they are actually in Cleveland. This visit might help explain a few things."

Fish continued with his questions. "You wouldn't know anything about Christina and Alan Blackridge disappearing together, would you Milt? You say you haven't heard from Christina since she disappeared?"

Milton's eyes wandered over to the Sheriff as he asked, "Sheriff, if they really went to Cleveland, how would you know they are still there…after all, that was a long time ago, and the letter saying they intended to go to Cleveland was never delivered, right? Maybe they changed their minds? It's been quite a while since they disappeared. Both Allen and Christina could be in Timbuktu by now, don't you think?"

Fish responded in a slow and deliberate manner. "You're right Milton, they could be anywhere…who knows…a lot closer to home, maybe…like Lacey Woods?"

"What do you mean by that, Sheriff? What are you trying to imply?"

"I'm just trying to connect the dots, Milton. The kids find a letter that was never delivered, written by a man that mysteriously disappears, and this letter is contained in the back pocket of a pair of jeans that were buried near a human bone…well…dot-to-dot-to-dot. Is it possible that the man who mysteriously disappears, and the jeans and the bone are connected?"

Milton was quick to see where the Sheriff was going with this line of questioning.

"It's been so long, Sheriff, and I can't really remember what it was like being young, when I married Christina. Sure did love that girl, you know…but I never was a jealous man. She was a good woman…kind, intelligent, and patient with me. She never complained about my pathetic efforts to support the family…working odd jobs on the bean farms, repairing combines, threshing corn, and then driving gondola rigs over to the silos in Fairfield. None of it paid very much."

As he listened, Fish slipped Milton a few sideways glances, Then he said "Well Milton, that's all history now. But what is history, really? Something that happened a hundred years ago…or something that happened yesterday? Seems like we have to write our own history, usually with the choices we make every day…you know?"

"Sheriff…I'm not a young man anymore…and I never had much luck when it came to making a living." Milton paused into silence.

The Bone

93

Fish glanced over at Milton and replied, "I can understand that, Milton. I grew up in these parts on a farm, on land my dad rented, and he could never really turn an extra dollar. Then one year, my dad couldn't make the rent, so he lost the farm, and then my Mom died. That's why I ended up in the military. When I got back from Korea, I never went back to farming. I couldn't go back. I joined the Police Department over in Fairfield ."

"So you never did get married?"

"No, never really had the time… or maybe it was that I never took the opportunity, which is more like the truth. After my Mom left us, it seems like staying together with a woman for any length of time just wasn't in the cards I was holding."

Milton began to feel less sleepy and he ruminated in a soft voice "Christina left me shortly after I bought the new truck and started making my round trips to Texas. I guess she had a tough time keeping to herself and all. I never really blamed her."

Milton placed his hands on his face and began to rub his temples slowly, eyes closed. Then he folded his hands in his lap and looked over at Fish. He began to speak from a heart filled with reflection.

"You seem to know how it is, Sheriff. You seem like a man who knows himself pretty well." He continued softly, "but it's only when you get old…that you really get to know yourself…who you really are, and not just who you pretend to be…I mean…who you've been in the past, and who you are…right now…here… and now…do you get me?"

"Yeah, Milt, I think I do. I think that our lives start out like jig saw puzzles…a thousand pieces of a story that we make up for ourselves, and as we grow up, we keep trying to piece our way to some picture of ourselves that seems to be good enough…not perfect mind you…but good enough to keep us going somewhere. But then there comes a point when we realize that many of the pieces we put in place are just not in the right places…the picture is not going to look like the cover on the puzzle box…and that's when the story goes from being a book of fiction, into a book of non-fiction…the illusion dissolves into the reality…and that can be hard to live with." A renewed silence descended on both men.

Then Milton let out a heavy sigh "I hope those kids haven't crashed my truck. I have to make a run down to Texas this week to pick up some auto parts. I've been hauling a lot of this stuff over to Lordstown. Gotta keep the line running over there," he explained.

It was well past four in the morning when the lights of Cleveland could be seen growing brighter as the near empty highway started to gather more cars, as well as trucks, heading into the city. A large gas station was tucked into a shallow bend in the road, and Sheriff Fish pulled in. He thought it might be a good idea to get some gas and talk with the help there to see if they had noticed any teenagers driving an eighteen wheeler, while Milton could check out a few rigs that were parked alongside the back of the station, and get himself a coffee.

Back on the road, the Sheriff entered Cleveland and headed for the northeast side of the city center, into the Industrial Valley neighborhood. Crossing over the Cuyahoga River, he found the corner of Euclid Avenue and 29th Street, and a long two story building with a sign in large black letters *"Blackridge Bakery. Home of Justin the Bagel King."* It was just past 5:30 in the morning, and a half-dozen panel trucks were idling in the parking lot, loading up before setting out on their morning deliveries. Perusing the parking lot, he saw no signs of Milton's truck.

Fish parked his squad car on 29th Street. "Let's go over and meet Justin," he said. He and Milton walked over and entered the building.

The bakery was filled with the tremendous aroma of doughnuts, bagels and rye breads, surrounded by the warmth of a dozen or more baking ovens and bubbling cauldrons of oil, all tended by watchful bakers, men and women, in white uniforms and aprons, heads covered with white caps.   Motion was everywhere. Bagels and doughnuts rolling down automated steel conveyor belts; flour and yeast, water and eggs, twirling in steel mixing machines and transferred to sheeting machines; flat sheets of finished dough sliding through stamping machines to render precise cutting of center holes. The marvelously automated processes that produce the simplest of joys: bagels and doughnuts.

As they entered, a young woman in business attire stepped forward from behind a receptionist desk and welcomed them.

 "How can I help you gentlemen?" Milton took a step back behind the Sheriff. The woman noted Fish's uniform and asked, "How can I help you, officer?"

"Hello. My name is Ray Vistifish. I'm the Sheriff of Rayford County, here in Ohio." Fish then quickly displayed his 5-pointed badge, and continued, "I'm conducting a small investigation for the county, and I wonder if I might speak with Justin Blackridge, if that's not too much trouble?"

The woman nodded her head slowly while a small look of concern crossed her face.

"I'm sorry," she said, "but Mr. Blackridge is not in his office now. He usually arrives around 7:30, sometimes later. You're welcome to come back."

"That would be fine," said the Sheriff, "I'll look forward to seeing you again."

With that, the Sheriff and Milton left the bakery. Fish noticed a small group of people entering a small diner near the end of the street. He decided to ask Milton to stake out the parking lot of the bakery in case his truck showed up. With the start of the new day, he needed some coffee himself, so he walked down to the diner.

When Fish entered the Diner, he noticed a group of four Latinos seated on the stools at the front counter, heatedly discussing something in Spanish, a language he did not know well. The counter lady was also Latino and busy, filling up their coffee cups and occasionally shaking her head aggressively at a young man the others in the group called Paco. Paco was dressed more elegantly than the other men, who were attired in blue jeans and hoodies. He seemed to be the one who was directing all the conversation, and the one who most likely was paying for everyone's breakfast. The counter lady had a deep frown on her face when Paco slipped her a twenty dollar bill as she filled his cup, and she spoke to him with impatience in a loud voice "*dejalos en paz*" and walked away. At this, the men seemed to withdraw from the discussion, and Paco quickly left the diner.

Fish looked down the row of booths along the front windows and was surprised to see Lucy Adams and Ms. Penquill quietly sharing a plate of pancakes. He concluded that the two women came to Cleveland for much the same reason as he did: to find their students. Fish walked over and looked at them with his head bowed.

"Very nice to see you ladies," he said. "I didn't expect to find you here in Cleveland, Ms. Adams. But I know how you feel about your students. I just didn't know you liked pancakes!" Lucy smiled gently at this observation and slid over towards the window, "Hello Sheriff, please sit down with us?"

Fish sat down next to Lucy and smiled at Ms. Penquill, who welcomed him with a grateful handshake. "Sheriff, I am worried sick about those two kids, and the thought that each of them is trying to find their missing parent will not let go of me. I want to help them in any way I can!"

"I can certainly appreciate that Ms. Penquill," replied Fish. "But … I .."

"Please call me Abigail, Sheriff," she interrupted…"Erin and Sinker have missed a lot of school this year, and I was looking forward to helping Erin study Shakespeare this summer."

Fish could see the tension in Abigail's face, and wanted to dispel some of the anxiety that was overwhelming her.

"Abigail, I don't know what will happen here. I will do my best to find those two, and find their parents, if they are here. But I have to tell you, we are in the early stages of this investigation, and there are still quite a few pieces of this puzzle I am missing. I am sure you will be a great help to everyone involved."

Lucy nodded at Fish, as she took a sip of her coffee. "I heard what the counter lady said to that man, the well dressed one, the one in a suit, just before he left. She said "*dejalos en paz*".

Fish recalled that Lucy was good with Spanish, discussing school matters with the many Latino farm families who had children in school. A sense of optimism was beginning to take root in his investigation, and he knew from experience that optimism is the most important element in solving any case. He felt encouraged that Lucy was here.

Lucy continued, "the man seemed angry with someone…or frustrated with something…"*Dejalos en Paz"* means "*Leave them alone.*" While I couldn't hear much of what the other men were saying, they all appeared to be a little worried at what the man in the suit was talking about."

Fish carefully logged in this new piece of information as another piece in his fact gathering.

"Thanks for the translation, Lucy" he said. "And I agree with you, the counter lady didn't look happy. Neither did any of the others. I wonder if me wearing my Sheriffs uniform had anything to do with that?" Fish said this with a small laugh. "Their discussion seemed to break up fairly soon after I walked in." Lucy and Abigail also laughed knowingly at this, realizing that this sort of occurrence was part of Fish's job, and must frequently happen to him. Rising from the booth, Fish quietly thanked them again for coming to Cleveland, and excused himself, citing the need to check in with the local police and make a few telephone calls. He agreed to join up with them again at the bakery a little later in the morning, and headed outside, down the street and back to his cruiser.

TWENTY-TWO

Square Zero

Sheriff Vistifish spent the remainder of the morning on the telephone with the London, Ohio, Missing Persons Division of the Bureau of Criminal Investigations (BCI). Most of his time was spent on the telephone discussing the forensic analysis of the bone found in Lacy Woods. He was finally getting some answers that would provide him with a path forward in the case:

1. The bone was carbon-dated as approximately 5 to 10 years old.
2. The bone was the femur from an adult male, approximately 20-40 years old.
3. The shoe was a size 10 leather work boot, commonly worn by farmers.
4. The soil residue on the boot was typed as limestone, commonly found in certain areas of southern Ohio where limestone bedrock is present, enriched with a significant accumulation of calcium carbonate. Soil structure was granular, with a pH of 7. The sample soil from Sam Hutchin's farm precisely matched the soil on the soles of the boot.
5. There were fingerprints on the buttons of the shirt that were not matchable in a data base search, but were distinct and well-preserved as evidence.
6. The tag on the blue jeans displayed the Great Zace Overall Company branding, which is the only denim

producer in Ohio. These jeans were size 33 and commonly worn by the farm workers in the state.

Sheriff Fish considered this information with concern. He had served as the Sheriff of Rayford County for over 25 years, and in that time period, he had referred only two people to the Missing Persons Bureau: Alan Blackridge and Christina Gilmer. And the bone was judged to be from a male, and the jeans in which the letter was found were a common size worn by a male. And the letter found in the back pocket of the jeans was written by Alan. And because the jeans were found together with the bone, he believed whoever owned the jeans also owned the bone.

Sheriff Fish slowly contemplated this dilemma:

Could the jeans belong to Alan, who then mysteriously disappeared before he was able to give the letter to Juan Benitez for delivery, as intended in the P.S. of the letter? Alan was still missing, and possibly dead.

Or could the jeans belong to Juan Benitez, the intended courier, who slipped the letter into his back pocket but failed to deliver it to Justin ?

The dirt on the boot perfectly matched the dirt on Sam Hutchins farm, where both men had worked. And before leaving for Cleveland, he had been sure to interview Sam Hutchins about Benitez, and was told by Sam that Juan Benitez was alive and well, and had quietly left the Lacey Woods Farm a long time ago, returning to Mexico to care for his mother.

If this was true, and Benitez was still alive, the soiled pair of jeans must belong to Alan.

The sheriff realized that he only had a theory here. At this stage of his investigation, he knew that the bone, and the collection of clothing, did not represent conclusive evidence that Alan was indeed dead; nor did it implicate Milton Gilmer of anything. At this point, all his theories were only unfounded hunches. And besides, he did not know for sure that Alan Blackridge wore jeans of size 33 and boots of size 10. All this would have to be verified in the course of his investigation. But most importantly, he did not know if Alan Blackridge was in fact dead, but instead was still alive somewhere, like Milton had suggested. Maybe both Alan and Christina were indeed alive and well in Timbuktu. Fish had been a Sheriff for a long time, and participated in many criminal proceedings and jury trials, and he knew a case like this would require rigorous proof, and evidence of a murder; evidence that would be convincing to jurors, beyond a reasonable doubt. In this case, he did not even have a key legal element: an identifiable body. He needed proof that someone was actually killed. All he had was an unidentified bone.

In addition, he realized he would need a defendant, someone who had the motive and opportunity to murder Alan. His suspicions about Milton Gilmer continued to grow in his mind, since the letter in the jeans verified that Alan had a romantic relationship with Milton's wife, and that Christina might be in danger too. He remembered that Milton had stated he was not a jealous man, which underscored his need to locate Erin and Sinker, and determine if they had found their missing parents still alive.

 Sheriff Fish returned to Justins' Bakery later that afternoon to continue gathering the information he would need to substantiate his theory. But after speaking with Justin, who had offered no information on the whereabouts of his brother Alan, he felt no closer to getting the answers he needed. But he was encouraged to find Erin, Sinker and Trip, as well as Lucy and Abigail somberly snacking on cream cheese and bagels in the company lunch room. They all felt like they were returning to square zero: Sinker had returned the truck to his dad Milton, who quickly departed, while Lucy was ready to take Abigail and her students back to New Canaan. They all seemed to accept the fact that they would soon be returning home without the parents they had been so hopefully expecting to find. After all these years, and all their hopes, nothing seemed to have changed.

As Lucy arrived with the teens back at Erin's house, she noted the excitement that had taken everyone by surprise before they travelled to Cleveland, and then the profound disappointment that silenced everyone on the car trip back home. She described the day they had spent in Cleveland to Erin's mother and related the misfortune of not having located the missing couple. Susan had expected this, and did not appear to be surprised. At the end of this long day everyone was ready to crash. Sinker seemed to displace his disappointment by slowly receding into his bubble, and Erin maintained her hopefulness that, somewhere, the sun must be shining.

TWENTY-THREE

The Pitchfork

It was early evening in New Canaan, and the warm air that had gathered in the afternoon sun was slowly lifting. A cool gentle breeze surrounded the trees in Lacey Woods, uplifting and raffling the isolated leaves. Paco Sendero drove slowly, with his headlights off, crunching down the gravel road that led to the Lacey Woods farm. He was not surprised to see Milton Gilmer's tractor-trailer resting on the side of the road. There was no sign of Milton, but Paco assumed he was nearby, talking with Sam Hutchins, since Milton had smuggled several truckloads of workers to Sam's farm over the past few months. It was good business for Paco. And Milton was a reliable driver.

As he entered the gate to the farm, he could hear voices in the barn. He walked inside slowly, keeping his left hand close to his side, cradling his handgun. Paco had never needed to use a gun in his work, but kept it near for any personal emergency that might arise. He could not imagine having to actually shoot someone. His only thought was to take care of his mother by sending her the money he earned. He justified his role as a human trafficker by believing that he was giving freedom to people who lived in desperate poverty and constantly contended with injustice…young men, like himself, who would face death or enslavement by the gangs. Just as he was. He was offering each immigrant a chance at a better life, and because there was also a chance that they might die in this process, he felt a great compassion for them. He was pleased to be working with Milton, and was impressed with Milton's refusal to transport women and young children, but only able-bodied men who were willing to work hard, and someday become United States citizens. And Milton transported immigrants only to farms in Ohio, and to farmers that he knew were respected in the community.

Once inside the barn, Paco saw Milton and Sam talking with a couple he did not recognize, sitting on aluminum lawn chairs. Milton and Sam looked up and instantly greeted Paco.

Sam then smiled and said, "Paco, I want you to meet Alan Blackridge. He used to work for me a long time ago, as a crew leader." Then he looked over at Christina and continued, "This is Christina, Milton's ex, I guess? These two ran away together years ago. It didn't make sense to me at the time, Alan just up and quit, and they ran off together…and after you left Alan…Milton became the man who would bring me the additional field hands, the immigrants I needed each season, mostly from Mexico, you know… undocumented, no work visas, that kind of thing." He paused, then resumed, "I didn't enjoy doing this at the time, but Amos Kingsbury and I needed the workers. Looking back, I knew it was wrong but I've reached an understanding with myself. Now, I think it's probably the right thing to do…anyway, I'm not concerned about myself anymore. I'm concerned for these immigrants." As Sam spoke, Paco nodded his head slowly.

Sam continued, "Milton has been filling me in on everything that's been happening lately. Paco, I think we may have a problem. You see, while Milton was up in Cleveland yesterday, the County Sheriff was there as well, looking around for these two," pointing at Christina and Alan. It seems Christina's boy and Alan's little girl somehow dug up a bone over in the woods a week ago, a human bone, and some old clothing, and the Sheriff is thinking it belongs to Alan, here. You see, Sheriff thinks he was murdered by somebody, since neither Christina nor Alan have been seen around here for quite a while. Milton has the feeling that Sheriff has tagged him as the prime suspect… that he killed Alan out of jealousy. Yet the Sheriff doesn't *really* know who that bone belongs to, does he?... but he's working on it, and he aims to find out… I'm pretty sure he thinks Milton wanted revenge for Alan running off with his wife, so he murdered Alan, and dumped him in the Woods."

At hearing this, Alan's face twisted slowly in a look of disbelief, while Christina had a look of puzzlement.

Alan said, "I knew the Sheriff and my daughter Erin were there in Cleveland looking for me…and Christina. Milton… your boy Thaddeus was there, too ...my brother Justin told me. But Justin wasn't sure what it was all about, so he wouldn't talk to the Sheriff." Then he looked squarely at Milton.

"Milton, you *have* to be the prime suspect because Christina and I fell in love, she leaves you, and then you made threats against us. When Christina and I disappeared…well, it all makes sense. That's why the Sheriff wants to find me so badly, so he can knock down his own theory, and find out why that bone was buried in Lacey Woods and who it belonged to."

Sam Hutchins chuckled under his breath and said "I really feel sorry for the Sheriff…he's gonna have a hard time pursuing this once he learns you're still walking around, Alan…and if you want to hang this on Milton, you and Christina will have to disappear again, maybe for good?"

At this, Alan jumped up from his chair. "No way! When the Sherrif was up in Cleveland yesterday, my brother told me he was trying to find out where I was, but Justin refused to tell him anything. But when Justin told me he was also looking for my daughter and her friends, I realized I needed to be back with my daughter…and Christina wants to be back with her boy. That's why we came back, so the Sheriff will find me, and we can stay here with our children. So the Sherrif will just have to find somebody else who owned that bone, and the somebody else who put it in the ground." He continued, "I can think of other possible suspects." Then Alan directed his next words to Sam.

"Sam, I once worked for you and Amos Kingsbury. You both have land right next to each other, and usually have high-yielding operations, almost every year. I know you need lots of farm hands that you can't find around here in New Canaan. So where do you get them?"

Sam began to look more concerned as Alan looked at him more intently.

Sam responded to Alan's question by looking at Paco and Milton. "Well it's true I have always needed some extra help. And I know that Amos is always short-handed since his son moved away to Toledo."

Alan interrupted, "…and does Milton deliver some of this extra help?"

"Well sure... I have an understanding with Paco. Paco gives me a call and sets me up with Milton."

Alan countered…"Do these workers have H-2A work visas?"

"Well….no…you have to understand…that takes too much time and causes too many problems. First of all, I have to complete an H-2A visa petition with U.S. Citizenship and Immigration Services. Then the workers are required to apply for the H-2A visa with the Department of State and complete consulate interviews in their home country. All this must be completed at least 45 days before they can start work. The problem is…I don't always know when I'm gonna need them, and how many I'm gonna need. Then I am responsible for the travel costs, medical costs, food and living quarters, these expenses can dig a big hole in my operation. And besides, approved workers are required to travel to the farm and arrive on the start date and be documented with an arrival and departure record. And if they can't be found on their departure date, I can get into big trouble."

Alan nodded. And he knew from experience that many workers leave mid-season for other opportunities, such as higher-paying jobs or more stable employment. The turnover rate can be very high. No one knows where they go, and they are the responsibility of the farm operator. He smiled gently at Sam and said " I can see why you don't want to get involved with the H-2A visa program. You could end up facing a lot of legal and financial liability."

Sam replied "You can see…with all the costs and record-keeping, it's much easier to get my help from Paco. I'll take my chances with him." Sam gave Milton and Paco a quick reassuring glance. Then he turned back to Alan. "Look Alan…me and Amos are just legacy farmers…you know…we have "family farms". We struggle every year to compete with the "Big Ag" corporations and depend on seed and pesticide suppliers like Monsanto. We have to keep our expenses as low as possible in order to remain the largest operators in this part of Ohio. If we don't succeed, we are gone."

Alan could see that the Sheriff would make sure all the dots were connected. He spoke with exasperation to Sam. "Sam, I think I understand. But I can also see that once the Sheriff learns me and Christina are still alive, the Sheriff won't have any trouble connecting the bone he found to other suspects, like Paco, and the farmers involved with him…that means you and Amos. Rather than go through all the financial and legal headaches, isn't it much easier to make an illegal farm worker just disappear? Like he had never been on your farm in the first place? No muss, no fuss, right?"

Paco didn't like the sound of this, of course, but he considered the role he played in the labor shortage problem less complicated than Sam's. Financially it was simpler and more rewarding. His gang recruited the workers, collected the money and put the workers on Milton's tractor-trailer. Milton just made sure the workers arrived….Point A to Point B, and then returned them to Mexico when they were no longer needed, Point B to Point A. And Paco knew the agricultural system the farmers had to struggle with would keep the demand for temporary immigrant workers steady. So Sam and Amos had big targets on their backs…they both arrange and pay for these migrants. If the Sheriff finds out that Alan is in town…well… for the Sheriff, their farms would be a good place to start investigating.

There was a heavy pause in the conversation, and a growing sense of unease on the faces of Paco and Milton. Alan looked somberly at Sam, and continued in a raised voice, "Since I am not the owner of the bone they found over in the Woods…Sam, whose bone is it? That's what the Sheriff is working to find out, and you can be sure Sheriff Ray Vistifish will never quit on this!"

Before Sam could answer, Milton broke the silence, "Paco, you'd better follow me back to my place and stay there tonight. We need to talk…the Sheriff will be heading this way soon. He'll be wanting to visit here with Sam, I am sure."

Sam added, "I think you're right Milton…I should have a talk with Amos, and make sure he's aware of everything."

TWENTY-FOUR

The Strangers

Alan and Christina parked outside Erin's home and sat in the silence of the darkened car. Before returning to New Canaan, they had discussed the problem of reappearing to their families after having been missing for such a long time. They could not think of any reasonable explanation that they could offer that would ease the pain and confusion that their departures had cost the children. At the time they met each other, the children were still quite young, and would not understand the strength of the attraction that drew them together. And Alan and Christina barely understood the consequences that would result from falling in love outside their marriages. They could not imagine the hopelessness and destruction that they had created. Is this what falling in love with each other can do? Or were they just being selfish, and disguising a fleshly attraction as love? How could they so carelessly abandoned their responsibility to their marriages and family? Can love create such lasting and deep pain? But lovers know better than anyone what the pain of separation can do. Abandoning their families for love demanded a high price.

They had no idea what would happen next, but they knew that they still loved their children and had no choice but to be with them again. So they walked up to the front door, and peered through the four small glass squares that lined the top of the door. And there they were, Erin and Sinker seated on the sofa, while Trip lay on the floor, with his arms spread out like the wings of a crow. Sinker had his arm protectively around Erin, as she lay her head, softly on his shoulder. Alan immediately recognized his little Erin…the same curious eyes and dusty blond hair that loosely circled around her narrow shoulders…and her smallish ears that leveled with the high arch of her cheekbones. Christina was startled by the changes in her boy Thaddeus, who she had not known as 'Sinker'. His hair was darker and thicker than before, and curled closely around his ears, providing a compatible background for his deep brown eyes. She did not remember the intensity resting in those eyes when he was a boy, but realized her boy was now almost a man.

Alan squeezed Christina's hand and quickly knocked on the door. He did not want to miss this moment.

At the sound of the knock, Trip took flight. He bounded up from the floor and peered back through the small glass squares, but in the darkness, he did not recognize the couple. But Erin had the immediate intuition that it must be her father. Had the Sheriff found him and told him that she had travelled to Cleveland to find him? Had the Sheriff found him and brought him back home? She rushed to the door with a high-pitched yelp, gently tugging on Trip to move so she could let the strangers in.

As Alan stepped into the home, Erin rapidly back-pedaled toward Sinker, who had opened his arms to receive her, and protect her from this stranger. In complete disbelief, Sinker saw his mother enter the house behind Alan. He released Erin and rose off the sofa, as if gravity had reversed itself and was pulling him irresistibly onward, his eyes locked on Christina. Christina stumbled and knelt on the floor with her arms covering her face to hide the tears. Sinker felt that he would somehow collapse back into his time bubble, and his voice dropped into a low whisper, as if he were talking to himself once again, but he could only say one word, "mother!". As they embraced, Sinker struggled his way back out of his time bubble, and Erin could see him crying, with his head pressed closely next to his mother's shoulder, tightly surrounded in his mother's long hair. Christina rocked him in her arms, slowly back and forth, with a gentle whispering, "Thaddy, Thaddy, I'm really back."

Alan approached the sofa where Erin sat, her hands cupped around her mouth and eyes. He held his arms wide open as if they were wrapping themselves around a heavy weight, as if he were struggling to pick her up from a fall, like he did when she was a toddler. It had been that long. In an instant, Erin's arms responded to her memories, and fixed themselves tightly around her father. Her tears testified that Alan was the father that she would not forget. The bond had not been broken.

Trip observed his friends in quiet admiration. He had never been without a parent, because all tribal members are considered your parents and are responsible for all the young. They understood that "it takes a village" to raise good children. Trip had often marveled at the white man's culture, and how impractical it seemed when it came to raising children.

Tonight, with the return of Sinker's mom and Erin's dad, Trip could clearly see how badly Erin and Sinker needed the village. He could feel deeply in his spirit that this room was being renewed and filled with joy, and a new beginning had arrived.

Standing by the open door, Trip saw Sheriff Fish's police cruiser stop behind Alan's car and Fish walking up to the house. Trip turned to Alan, "Mr. Blackridge, Sheriff Vistifish is here." Alan kissed his daughter tenderly on the forehead and sat her back down on the sofa. As Fish entered the room, Alan nodded and greeted him in a low voice. "Thanks for everything, Sheriff. It's good to be home again. As you can see, I am still alive." Fish glanced at the teens. " Lucy told me she had dropped everyone back here at Erin's house, and I had a hunch that you both got the news in Cleveland that we were looking for you. My experience told me that Justin knew more than he was willing to say. But I can see that everything is working out here Alan. I am especially glad to see you and Christina, both alive and back in New Canaan. For a while…well…I thought something bad might have happened to you."

Trip saw this as an opportunity to tell the Sheriff about Milton, and pulled Fish aside to reveal some of the things he had witnessed at Sinker's house, about the gun and the large amount of money Milton had displayed before the trip to Cleveland. Trip worried about Sinker and wanted the Sheriff to know.

Alan overheard this brief conversation, and stepped over to tell Fish about the talk he had earlier that evening with Sam.

Fish thanked them both, and said "I've had suspicions about Milton for some time, and now, it's late. I think its time to wrap this case up. I've been in touch with the FBI field office in Cleveland, and they sent some folks down to New Canaan. I need to talk with Sam Hutchins tonight, before they do." With that, the Sheriff left.

Overwhelmed with the tidal wave of emotions, Alan and Christina, like the good parents they hoped to be, wanted their children to get some quiet time. They promised the children that this would be the start of a new life, and they would return in the morning for a reunion breakfast. With that, they returned to their motel near Fairfield for the night.

Sinker and Erin soon spread out on the floor of Erin's home, speaking quietly with each other, comparing over and over their incredibly joyful thoughts of how their lives would now be changed in ways they could barely imagine.

Trip listened with eyes closed, reassured to hear the back and forth of their happy voices. Sinker talked about his mother as if she were his fairy godmother coming back to grant his wish. But his mood changed when he thought of his father. And this made sleep impossible. Erin reached out for Sinker's hand and asked him "Sheriff Fish probably will need to question your Dad about how he got all that money, and he probably knows why he has been hanging out with Paco. I think this could mean trouble for your Dad?"

Then Sinker rose up and spoke "Trip, we have to go back to my house and warn my Dad that the Sheriff knows all about the gun he has, and what he has been doing to get all that money… and by now, he probably plans to arrest him."

When Erin heard this, she also rose from the floor, and all three found their shoes quickly, then quietly opened the front door, and they were gone.

Fish drove slowly on his way through town, heading for Sam's farm. He made a stop at Abigail's house to check on her and reassure her that the students were well, and once again back home with their missing parents. Abigail was happy to hear the news that Alan and Christina were found, and were reunited with the kids. But she informed Fish that she had been disturbed by all the lights and noise coming from the heavy machinery operating in Lacey Woods, not far from her house.

"Yes, Abigail, I heard the loud noises coming from the Woods as I came over to see you. Let me update you on what's happening, but I have to ask you to keep this confidential, because it is part of the ongoing investigation." Abigail nodded in puzzled agreement.

Fish continued, "the Ohio Bureau of Criminal Investigation is working with the FBI. They have brought some people and earth-moving equipment to New Canann and have just begun excavating a large tract of ground in Lacey Woods. It seems that they have discovered more than just one bone. In fact, they have removed at least four skeletons buried over there… as of now."

Abigail drew in a quick gasp of air as her face recoiled in disbelief.

"They will be working around the clock for the next few days to determine the extent of any criminal activity. I am sorry for this inconvenience, Abigail."

"What do you think is going on?"

"I am not certain about all of this yet. But because I notified the Bureau of Missing Persons, and asked their forensics people to analyze the bone I sent them, they referred this to the Cleveland field office of the FBI. The FBI felt there was enough evidence to take a closer look. They are testing some of the bones they have found so far, and right now, it looks like they are relatively recent burials. Only five to ten years old. Nothing older than that. Homeland Security's Immigration and Customs Enforcement, as well as the Agricultural and Labor Departments are all very interested in this."

"I can't believe this is happening so close to my home, and right here in New Canaan?" Abigail responded with an air of dejection. "How can life get so complicated in our small town?"

She continued, "Please keep me informed, Ray", unusually addressing the Sheriff by his first name. Ray noted this and considered this as a reflection of how concerned she must be. He responded by holding her hand for a moment and said in a gentle voice, "Abigail, yes, I will keep you informed. Please don't let this worry you."

As the Sheriff drove his car past Lacey Woods, on the way to Sam's farm, the bright flood lamps arrayed around the trees drew his immediate attention. He saw men dressed in masks and white hazardous material uniforms searching for more bodies, digging with short-handled shovels or riding atop a backhoe. He slowly pulled his cruiser over to the FBI tent where he could see several agents sifting through steel drums filled with earth.

He parked and walked over to the tent. With a deep sense of concern that events may yet overwhelm him, despite his years of experience, he felt a cruel bewilderment pressing in on him as he realized the magnitude of the body count. "Evening, gentlemen. I'm Rayford County Sheriff Ray Vistifish, how are we doing in the ground here?"

"Good to meet you Sheriff. I'm Special Agent Joe Kirby. The Cleveland field office put me in charge of this dig. Can you tell us anything more you know about the bone you found, and how it got into this patch of woods?" His voice sounded fatigued, but Fish could see a look of professionalism in his eyes that is only developed over years of investigations.

Fish shook hands with Kirby and another agent working nearby. Fish thought for a moment, then responded.

"I think you all are ahead of me here. This all started when two of our local residents went missing about ten years ago. Back then…I made some inquiries…but nothing looked out of the ordinary. It was my opinion at the time that adults have the right to disappear if they want to. I couldn't find any evidence or reason to expect a crime. But I reported them as possible missing persons to the Missing Persons Bureau in Columbus. But a few days ago, when a couple of teenagers accidently dug up a bone and some other things, I've learned there was more to their disappearance. It's complicated."

"Most disappearances are complicated, even runaway teens" replied Kirby. "Sometimes, they are never found…but this is different," he said, gesturing to all the machinery rolling back and forth under the lights.

Fish nodded. "Well…the local folks who fell in love and disappeared ten years ago have returned, and provided me with some information that looks important. Tonight I'm on my way to visit one of our local farmers who may help us get to the bottom of all this."

Kirby looked very interested in obtaining this additional information.

"Do you want one of my agents to go with you?" he asked. "Maybe they can help?"

Fish looked around at the trees that were swaying back and forth as a back hoe moved across the various mounds of freshly excavated earth. Four black body bags were stacked neatly in an undisturbed patch of the Woods. A few empty bags lay on the ground nearby.

"No, Joe. I don't think that will be necessary. The people I'm dealing with here are long time residents in Rayford County…good people, really. I believe they will be more helpful if they talk with someone they have known for a long time."

"Sounds good to me, Sheriff. Just get back to me with anything that's important, OK?"

"Will do." At this, Fish returned to his cruiser, and carefully rolled down the road to Sam's farm.

TWENTY-SIX

Sam and Amos

When Fish arrived at Sam's farm, he slowly walked up to the barn, where Sam and Amos sat on the asphalt curtain in a pair of faded green aluminum lawn chairs. The light that hung from the top of the barn entrance illuminated them in a half shadow that came from the edge of the roof line.   Sam had an anxious look on his face as he acknowledged the Sheriff's approach, while Amos refused to meet the Sheriff with any type of greeting or eye contact. Fish guessed that the two had been sitting like this, talking with each other outside the barn, for quite some time. Maybe they had been waiting for him to arrive. He spotted another lawn chair, similarly made of aluminum that had the same weathered shade of red as the barn. Fish dragged it over to where Sam and Amos sat. The sound of the excavations emanating from the Woods was vibrant, almost mesmerizing for the two men, who sat blithely looking at a small sliver of moon slowly rising above an island of trees.

Sheriff Fish spoke first, interrupting their rural revery.

"Hello Sam...Amos... I guess Alan told you why I'm here? And you can hear for yourself what's going on over in the Woods."

Sam nodded to himself and adjusted his position to look more directly at Fish.

"Yes Ray…we've been expecting you." Amos remained silent, his eyes still fixed upwards at the sky.

"Sam…it's the FBI making all the noise over there in the Woods. I hate to mention to you that they have located four bodies…well…really skeletons…and they will be working through the night to see if they can locate any more." Sam's face remained unmoved by this information, as if someone were telling him something he already knew.

"Sheriff, I believe they will find two more, that's all. They were all immigrants that me and Amos needed these last few years to bring in the beans…ever since his son left the farm." As he spoke, Amos slowly lowered his head to see only his feet resting in the driveway. Sam paused to wait for the Sheriff's reaction.

Fish did not look at Sam, but simply lowered his head, without showing any hint of surprise. Then, in a low voice, he asked "How did this happen, Sam?"

Sam began to speak when Amos sharply interrupted him.

"Sam…what's the use? We've been on our land for over a hundred or more years…. Over that time we've seen more farmers lose their farms… their families…and their lives to the Banks and the government, who sell us out to Big Ag…the big corporations who come in with all their money, machinery and miracle seeds. We can't compete any longer. The only help we can get is from immigrants, and the government is cracking down on them…making it so damn hard to get work visas and so expensive to take care of them. Sam, let's face it, the days of the family farm are over. Over…that's all. We were part of a dream…Sam, and the dream…is over. Now…the earth and the rain and the sun belong to the factory farm, not the family farm."

Amos returned his head to its upward position, taking in the moon and the sky surrounding it, with a wistful stare. The dome of the universe seemed to close around all three men, the Sheriff, Amos, and Sam, and the night pushed down on each of them, with only the sound of crickets rising up from the fields.

Fish ruminated on what to say next. This did not look good for Sam and Amos, the two pillars of this farm community. He turned and slid his chair closer to Sam.

"Sam, I have known you longer than anyone else in New Canaan. I coached your son Carson at the high school. You donated the land for our football and baseball teams. You are the pillar of our community. I know you would never hurt anyone."

He looked over at Amos who added "and the Kingsbury family has been in Rayford County since before the Civil War." A look of dejection lingered over his face.

"What happened here Sam? These bodies were found on your property, and you know you are going to be the prime suspect."

Sam looked over at Amos, who quietly nodded to him and said "Tell him all about it Sam. It's mostly my fault. Since my wife died, and my son moved away, I don't have much of a future here on a farm. They're gonna take it away from me anyway."

Sam could see the despair in Amos's eyes, and he knew it was "time for truthin" as his father always said to him when he was a boy.

"Ray, you are the best Sheriff Rayford County has ever had since anyone can remember, and you had it rougher than some when you were a boy and your Mommy died. It was that flu that snuck up on her. It snuck up on all of us that year. I think they called it the 'swine' flu, even though we never raised any hogs around this area." He paused to straighten out his hands that were clenched with tension and knurled from seventy-five years of hard work.

"Well, it was in the fall of that year, I think it was '75 or '76, and the sheds where the farm workers from Mexico were living got awfully quiet. The men weren't coming out to the fields anymore, and they were good hard workers, even the younger ones. That didn't make sense. When I went to check on them one morning, I met with Alan Blackridge, who was my crew leader at the time, and he told me that more than half of the crew couldn't get out of their bunks. I entered one shed and found a young fella named Benitez covered with sweat and hacking half his lungs out. I remember the glassy look in his eyes like I never seen. He was a good boy, young and strong. Alan took care in passing out their wages every week, in little white envelopes. Alan told me that Benitez wanted to leave the farm, find better work elsewhere. But he was an *illegal immigrant.* I couldn't afford to get him an H-2A visa, and

I didn't want all the liability and fines that come with that. So one payday, Alan put a little extra money in the envelope he gave to Benitez, enough to get him to Cleveland and find a job with his brother Justin, who started a little bakery and needed extra workers. He also put a short letter in the envelope, addressed to his brother, vouching for the man as a hard worker. I gave my approval to Alan, since I thought Benitez would run away anyhow… he was young and wanted a better future. A runaway would be more trouble for me. More expense defending myself from the government. And besides, the boy had agreed to send back some money to cover his expenses at the farm."

Fish sat back in his lawn chair, and stared across the fields of soybeans in silence. In his mind, he began to put all the pieces together, one by one. He needed to reconstruct what he already knew about events, and try to answer any questions he had and close the gaps in what had really taken place.

So how did the letter from Alan end up buried in the back pocket of some jeans: Fish felt he finally understood how that letter ended up in the jeans: Fish figured that Alan was running away with Christina and wrote the letter requesting to stay with Justin in Cleveland. Alan also wanted to give a good recommendation for Benitez, who had agreed to deliver the letter. So the jeans must have belonged to Benitez. And the bone found by Erin and Sinker probably belonged to Juan Benitez.

But why wasn't the note delivered as planned? : Well, it didn't take 25 years of police work to figure that one out.

Benitez had died before he could make the trip…probably from the swine flu that was tearing up the entire farm community.

How was Benitez going to get to Cleveland? That's where Milton comes in. Sam must have arranged with Milton to carry him up to Cleveland on one of his runs.

So how did Benitez end up in the ground? : After Benitez died from the flu, Sam or Amos had someone in the family dispose of the body in property that he owned. Property that wasn't used for farming, and property that was out of the way and covered by trees that he could keep an eye on: Lacey Woods was a good place to hide something.

Why were so many other bodies buried in the Woods? : Probably his neighboring farmer and best friend Amos had the same problem. His farm hands were getting sick too.

And why weren't they receiving vaccinations or medical treatment? : Probably because the two farmers did not have insurance to cover them, or someone would find out that they were illegals, without documentation or H-2A visas.

Both Amos and Sam had now grown silent, politely sitting in their lawn chairs. Fish looked at them both with a look of sadness. He did not feel it necessary to press any more questions on these farmers. Except one.

"Sam, are you still receiving undocumented immigrants to help you on the farm?" He gave Sam an unexpected look of encouragement, knowing that the answer to this question might be the only way he could give him any help at all. If the answer was "no", then he might be able to get Sam a reduction in his sentencing by using him as a cooperative witness. If the answer was "yes", then he had given Sam a warning that the FBI was closing in on him. Sam thought for a moment, and then said one word.

"Yes."

Fish responded quickly, with two names, "Milton?...Paco?"

Sam nodded. To Fish, it all added up. *Two,* Sam and Amos, *plus two,* Milton and Paco, *can only equal four*.

This was the end of the discussion. As the Sheriff returned to the dig at Lacey Woods, he was sure that he had confirmed that *two, Erin and Sinker, plus three , Milton, Amos and Sam, equaled five.*

TWENTY-SEVEN

The Threshing

Trip, Sinker and Erin hurried down the road, stepping quietly and talking in soft whispers as they neared Sinker's house. They could see three black FBI vans parked along the side of the gravel road, in front of Milton's truck. Sinker noted that Sherrif Fish had parked his cruiser on the other side of the truck, and he must be somewhere near the house. Sinker counted six agents, some holding long guns, standing in the road. Special Agent Joe Kirby sat in the open front door of the lead van, talking into a walkie-talkie.

Trip knew the many different ways to enter Sinker's house without being seen, so he had everyone circle around to the back of the home and climb up the tree next to Sinker's second floor window. Once inside, they heard Paco and Milton planning their escape. Paco had darkened the house when he heard the vans coming up the gravel road, and continually peered through the window blinds. When he saw the teens coming down the stairs, he crouched behind the sofa, and pulled out his gun. He did not like being cornered, and he had never had to fight his way out.

Paco pointed his gun at Trip and spoke in a low but demanding voice, "how did you kids get in here?"

Trip replied, "I can get you out of here, too, without them seeing you, but you have to put your gun away. There are six FBI agents waiting out there, and they'll be coming in here soon."

Paco put the gun back in his coat pocket. "OK, just get me out of here."

Trip looked at Milton, "are you coming out too? We'd better go… now!"

Milton shook his head. "no…this is my house, and I am not leaving." Sinker seemed pleased to hear this, but he was surprised to realize how much he still cared about his father.

Trip led Paco up the stairs and showed him the open window in Sinker's room, near the tree limb. "You have to make a small jump here," he said. "Just grab the branch and climb down. It's strong enough to hold you. Then you can make your way to the highway. Just stay off the gravel road…they are all waiting out there."

Paco was not used to climbing down large trees in Mexico, since his little village was hot and dusty, with vegetation that was mostly stunted bush. But Paco sensed it was the only safe way out. Trip heard the FBI agents scrambling down the gravel road, approaching the house. He helped Paco get through the open window, and in a loud voice, yelled "Jump!" Paco obeyed. Alerted by Trip's yelling, Sheriff Fish had quickly positioned himself by the side of the house, watching for any attempted escapes. Moments later, Paco was apprehended and taken away in handcuffs.

When Trip returned down the stairs, Erin and Sinker were anxiously talking with Milton, urging him to leave the house . But there was no time left for discussion. It would be only a matter of seconds before the FBI came crashing through the front door.

When he heard the crackle from Agent Kirby's walkie talkie, Milton knew it was too late. Kirby and two other agents had ripped the front door off its hinges and stood with guns pointing at Milton. But Milton had his gun out, too, pointing it at Kirby.

"FBI!, FBI!" screamed Kirby. "Gilmer, drop the gun!...NOW!"

Milton quickly reached out to grab Sinker around the shoulders, and pulled his son close to him.

"I've got a few hostages here," he said, nodding his head in the direction of Erin and Trip. "So drop your weapons and sit on the sofa, if you don't want to see these kids get hurt." At this, the other agents looked at Kirby, who immediately lowered his gun, and positioned himself on the sofa.

Milton motioned to the teens to leave the house with him, and all four ran down the gravel road to Milton's truck. He opened the back doors of the trailer, and told them to quickly climb inside. Then he locked the doors. Sinker could not believe what his father was doing. The engine roared as Milton headed toward the highway, struggling to accelerate the heavy vehicle as quickly as possible, with the FBI vans rapidly following. The piercing high pitched sirens started softly, with their volume steadily increasing as they came closer and closer to Milton's truck. Milton was surrounded with the bright flashings from the syncopated strobe lights emanating from the pursuing vans, and reflecting off the large oblong side mirrors of the truck…staining the interior of the cab a deep vermilion and intermittently blinding Milton as he chaotically attempted to gain speed and keep his truck on the highway.

Inside the empty trailer, Trip told everyone to sit on the cargo floor near the wall of the trailer, but not to get too close to the sides. He knew that moving at this speed, the road was going to be rough, and in the dark insides of the trailer, he did not want Erin or Sinker slammed against the walls as the truck rounded a sharp bend in the road. Trip managed to grab one of the cargo ropes attached to the insides of the speeding truck and placed it around Erin and Sinker, who kept his arms wrapped tightly around Erin. In a shaky voice, barely audible above the loud high-pitched humming noises made by the rapidly rotating wheels of the trailer, Erin kept asking Sinker "where's your father taking us'?... why won't your father stop?" After each bump up and down, Erin curled up even more tightly against Sinker and whispered in his ear, "Sinker swim?...please…Sinker swim?...please…Sinker swim?" As she whispered this, she could feel her stomach twisting up and growing tighter with the pain. She thought of the amazing joy of finding her father this evening, something she thought would never possibly happen to her because he was supposed to be dead… and he would never come back… and now thinking…that she would lose him forever… because she was going to be dead… that she would lose him forever…and Sinker would lose his Mother forever…and now…knowing that she had found love with Sinker…and she was going to lose the first boy she ever loved…forever… was this how my life was supposed to end?

She mentally composed the final entry she would make in her diary, as the sounds of the FBI sirens were getting closer.

Dear Diary,

It's true. I know I should have made more time for you. But I was so excited to learn I might find my dad… I say 'might' because I think maybe he will not stay. Maybe this is all just a dream, or a nightmare. After all, I am in the back of a truck…but I have found Sinker, and we have been trapped, together, sliding around in this tractor-trailer, racing down a highway, travelling through the night. Each bump in the road is like a giant hand reaching out to wake me, telling me it is time to get up, and time to get away. But I don't want to leave Sinker. There is a rope, and we are tied together, and we will not be separated. He is the first boy I have ever loved, and I know he loves me too. And he has found his Mother! He has found his Mother! He has been released from his time bubble! He has found his freedom! My life is so unreal I can hardly live it… my life is so unreal…

As she tried to finish her thought, the giant hand reached out to grab her again, and twisted violently, shaking the truck. A fragment of missing asphalt on an unfinished piece of highway wrenched and bent the tires of the cab, flinging it sideways off the road unrestrained and slamming it against a bridge abutment, overturning the trailer onto its side with a furious twirling around in a tight circle, then coming to rest on its side. A dingy stream of smoke lifted upwards from the bottom of the cab, quickly growing thicker into a darkening thunder cloud that drifted back over the disabled truck.

The force of the impact against the bridge had flung open the rear doors of the trailer, as black smoke crept slowly into the trailer. Trip could feel the heat beginning to seep into the trailer from the newly kindled flames that flickered and darted up like lightning from the center of the smoke cloud , illuminating the cab with its blue and orange glow. Sinker and Erin were still bound with the rope Trip had lashed around them, suspended together, mid air, from the interior side of the truck that now served as the ceiling. Sinker hung on tightly to both the rope and Erin, while Trip untangled them and helped them escape from the trailer. Free from the truck, Erin held tightly to Sinker's hand.

The FBI vans pulled up behind the wreck and surrounded them in the glare of their headlights. They were no longer pointing guns at Milton, but instead were using their hands to shield their faces from the intense heat of the fire ignited by a crushed fuel tank. Sinker could see that the fire was spreading throughout the truck, and the heaviest black smoke was filling the cab where his father was slumped, without movement, across the front seat. The heat from the flames in the cab grew more intense and repressive, keeping the FBI agents from approaching the wreck and helping the unconscious man inside. Sinker thought of his father, lying unconscious in the cab, slowly losing life, trapped amid the smoke and the flames. All at once, he could feel his time bubble collapsing, dissolving in the heat of this present moment. Now he knew, this was the first day of his freedom, a freedom that would be never ending. His freedom. He ran toward the cab.

Erin could feel his surge of excitement as Sinker dashed towards the truck. Her eyes followed him as he ran through the thick haze of smoke and climbed into the cab until she could no longer see him. After several minutes, she knew that she would never see him again. She kept repeating to herself *my life is so unreal I can hardly live it... my life is so unreal ...* as if it were a mantra… and if only she kept repeating it and repeating it, it would somehow save Sinker. Trip stood next to her and saw the shock in her face sublimate into tears. He reached for her hand. But when he saw Sinker reappear on the step of the cab, he ran toward the smoke and flames. Sinker and Trip joined their arms together and lifted Milton's limp body free from the cab. They were joined by several FBI agents who quickly helped take Milton to the side of the highway. Milton was alive, but badly injured. Erin stood on the side of the road, huddled with Sinker and Trip, waiting for an ambulance, and watching the smoke gather into darkening clouds drifting upward into the star-filled sky. For the first time, Erin really believed…*somewhere... the sun must be shining.*

The Bone

136

1. Do you think that the absence of a mother is more painful for a child than the absence of a father?

2. Do you think Sinker is correct when he says "people are made to break rules, and rules are made to break people" ?

3. Why is Erin always telling Sinker "Sinker Swim" ?

4. What is motivating Sinker to remove all the mirrors in his house? What do the mirrors represent?

5. Do you think that at the time of the Civil War, the Northerners felt the Southerners were less educated and less interested in reading books?

6. Why was Sinker so intent on thinking about "Freedom", for himself and others, like the man who carved Freedom on the picnic table, and Triple Crow's grandparents? Freedom seems very important to Sinker. What does freedom mean to you?

7. Sinker believes that lying is not wrong, but just another way of seeing the world. Is he wrong?

8. Why does Milton feel his life is not turning out well? Is he correct that acquiring more money will make things better?

9. Why is Erin is so protective of Sinker?

10. Do you think that Paco was correct to join the gang to help his mother, or should he have gone to the local police instead to arrest the man who shot his father?

11. What does it mean to be a parent? What does it mean to be a child?

12. Are parents just two older people who live in the same place? And even if they live in the same house, do they really live in the same place?

13. What is history? Something that happened yesterday, or something that happened a hundred years ago?

14. Do you think that Sam Hutchins was right to hire illegal farm workers to help on his farm?

15. Do you think the H-2A Visa process that farmers must use to hire farm labor is too difficult and needs to be simplified, or do you think that immigrants who enter this country illegally should be arrested and deported? How would you address this issue?

16. Why did Sinker feel he had finally found his personal freedom when he escaped from the burning truck?